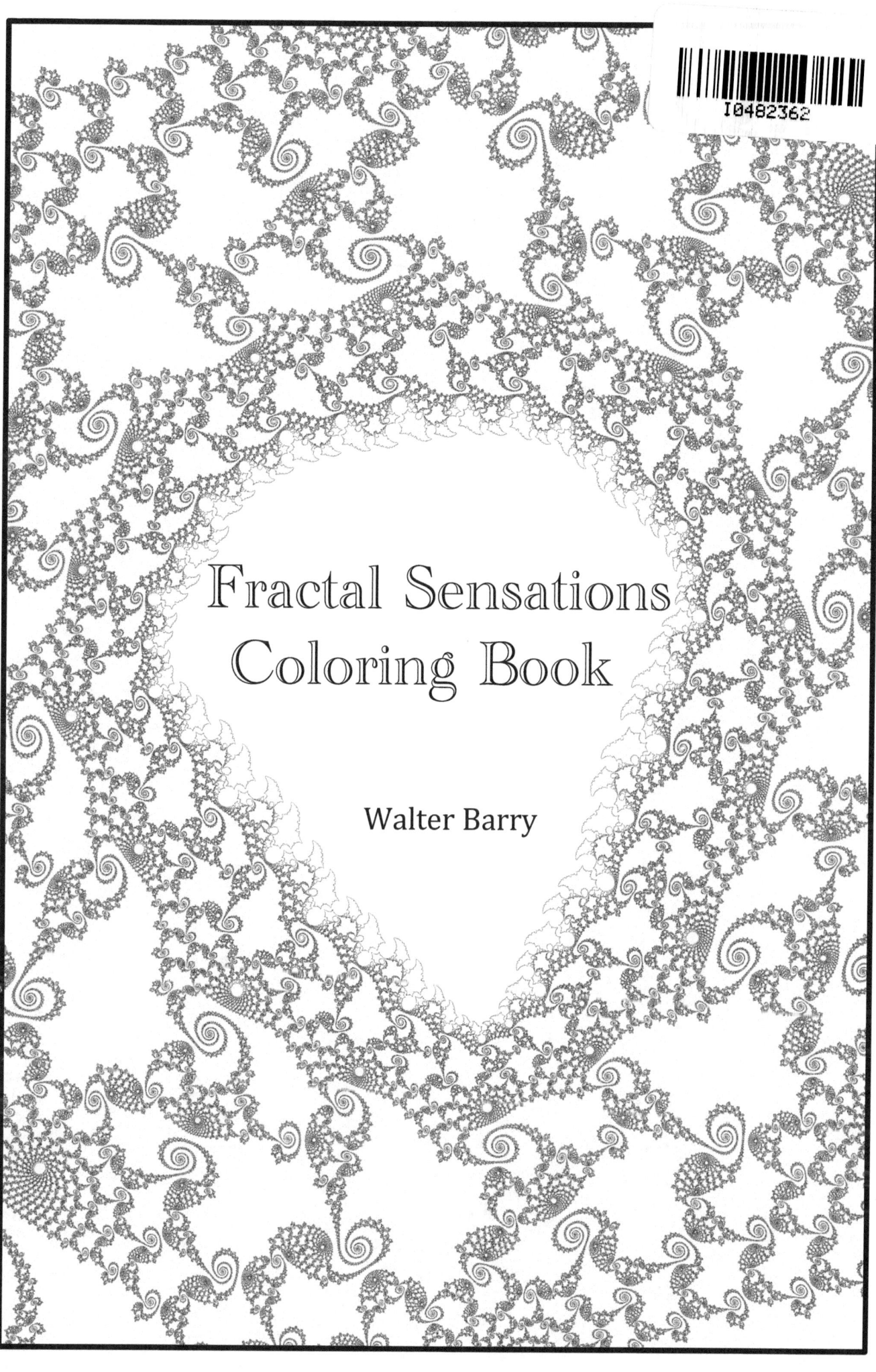

Fractal Sensations Coloring Book

Walter Barry

I0482362

Copyright © 2016 Walter Barry

All rights reserved.

ISBN: 1533504717
ISBN-13: 978-1533504715

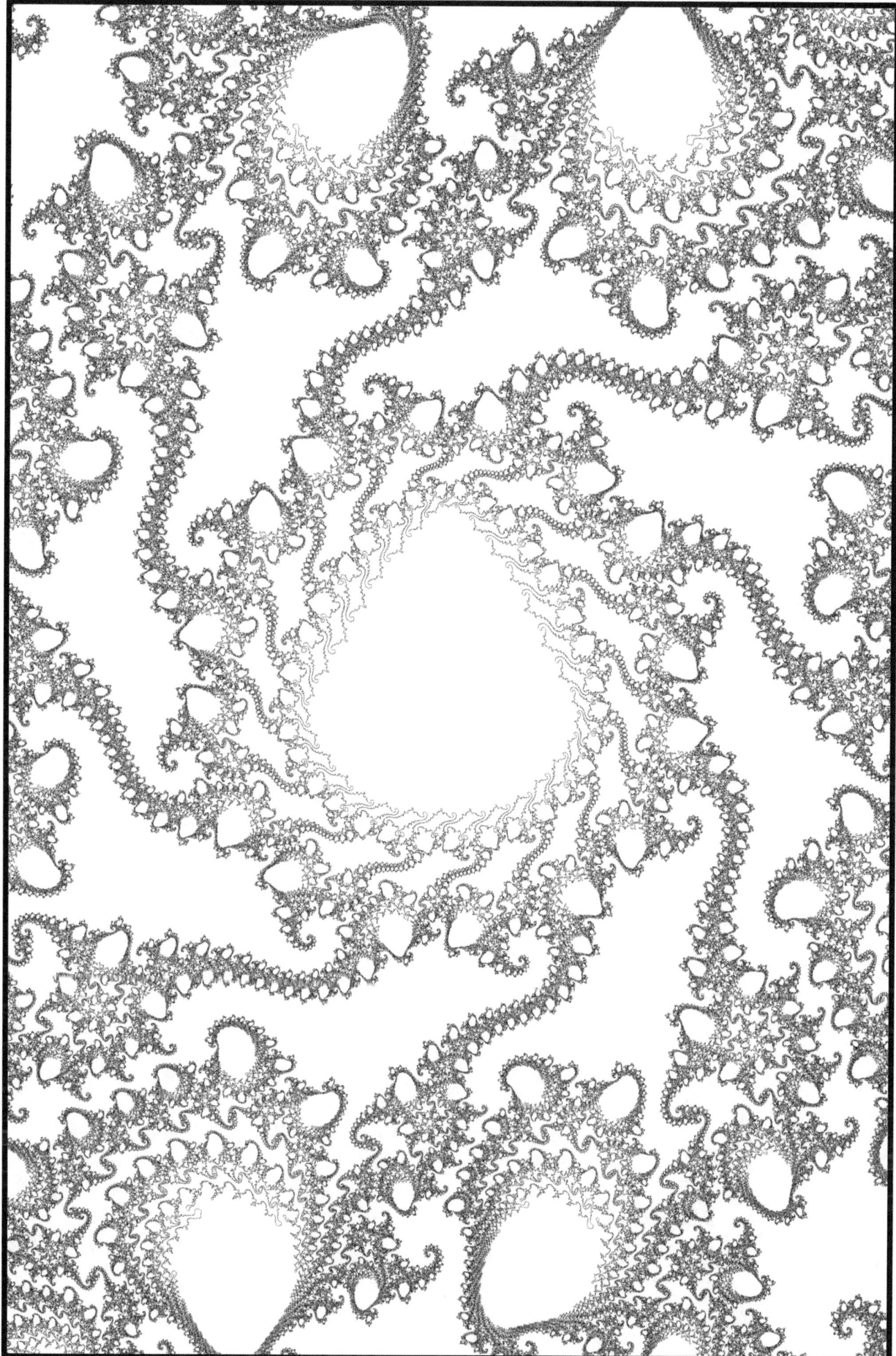

Gold Arms

Zoom: 7.320768359427133e-8,4.868596926533086e-8
Location: -0.7334321889358766,0.15081979761324818
Iterations: 810

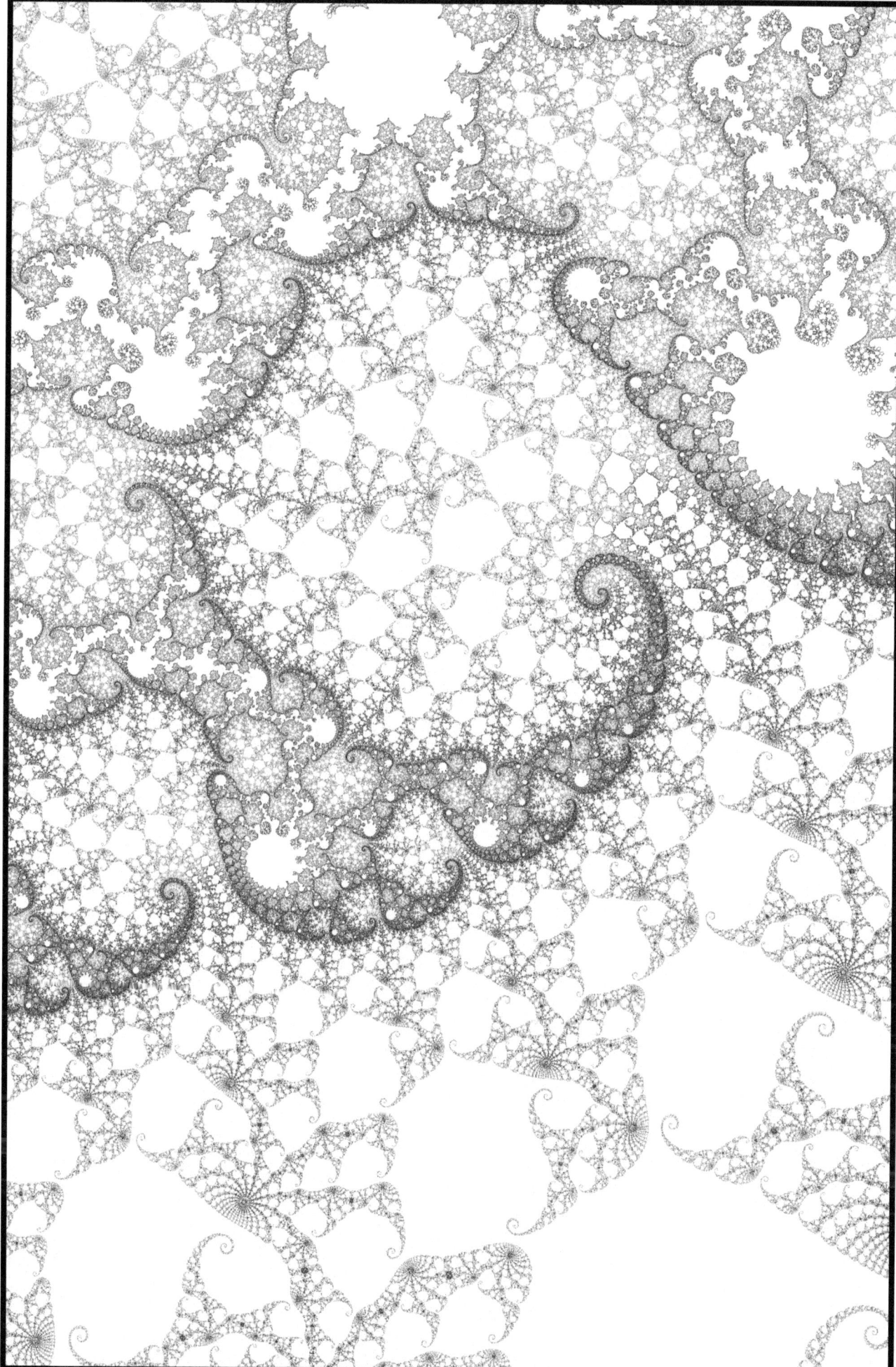

Broklee

Zoom: 4.582838964324442e-9,2.875677172318413e-9
Location: 0.2717332915585907,0.004893582589873648
Iterations: 2200

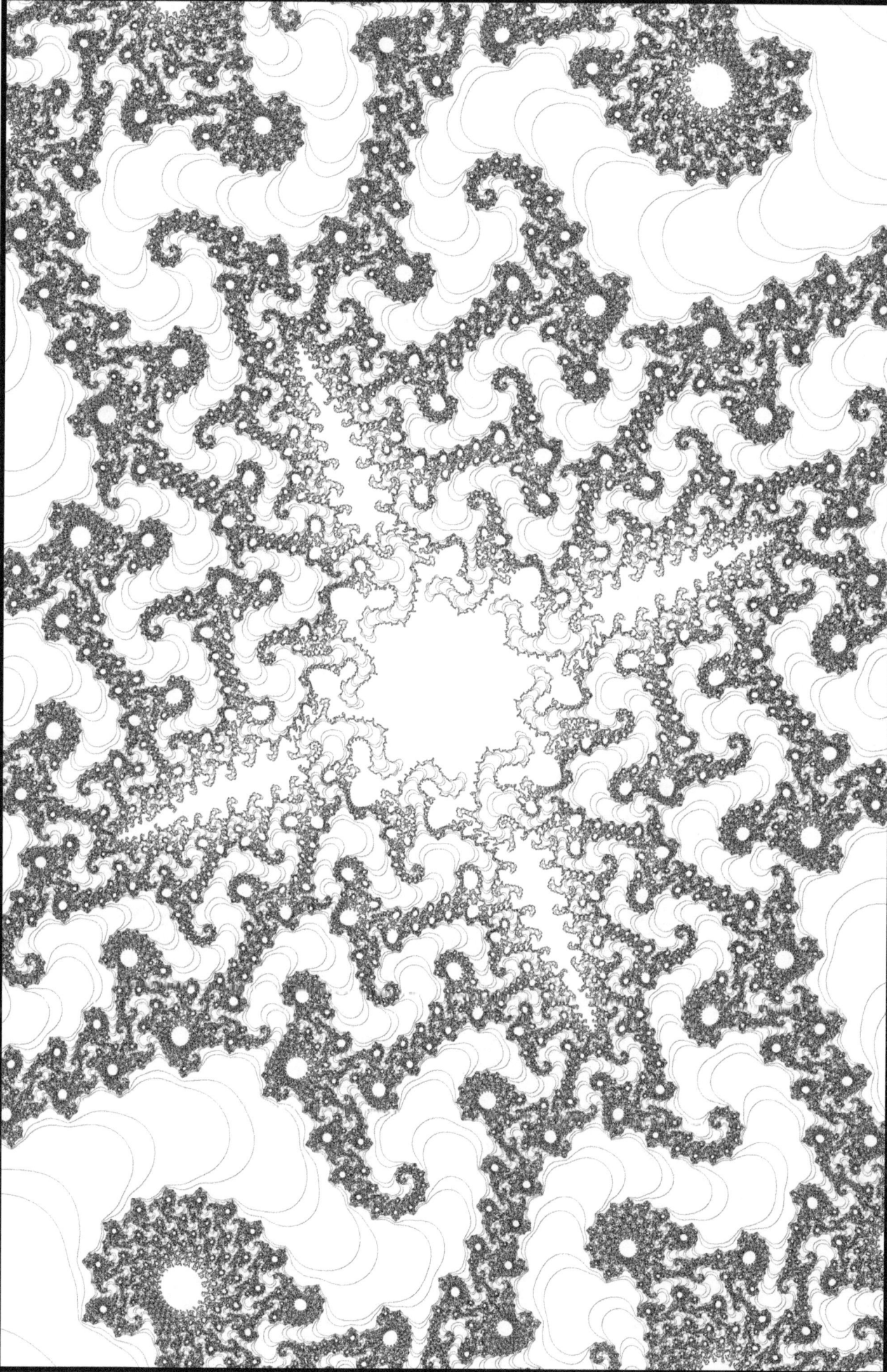

Julia Four Star

Zoom: 1.1992379800396153e-9,7.525076361910052e-10
Location: -0.7410827063826703,0.15786379589932706
Iterations: 484

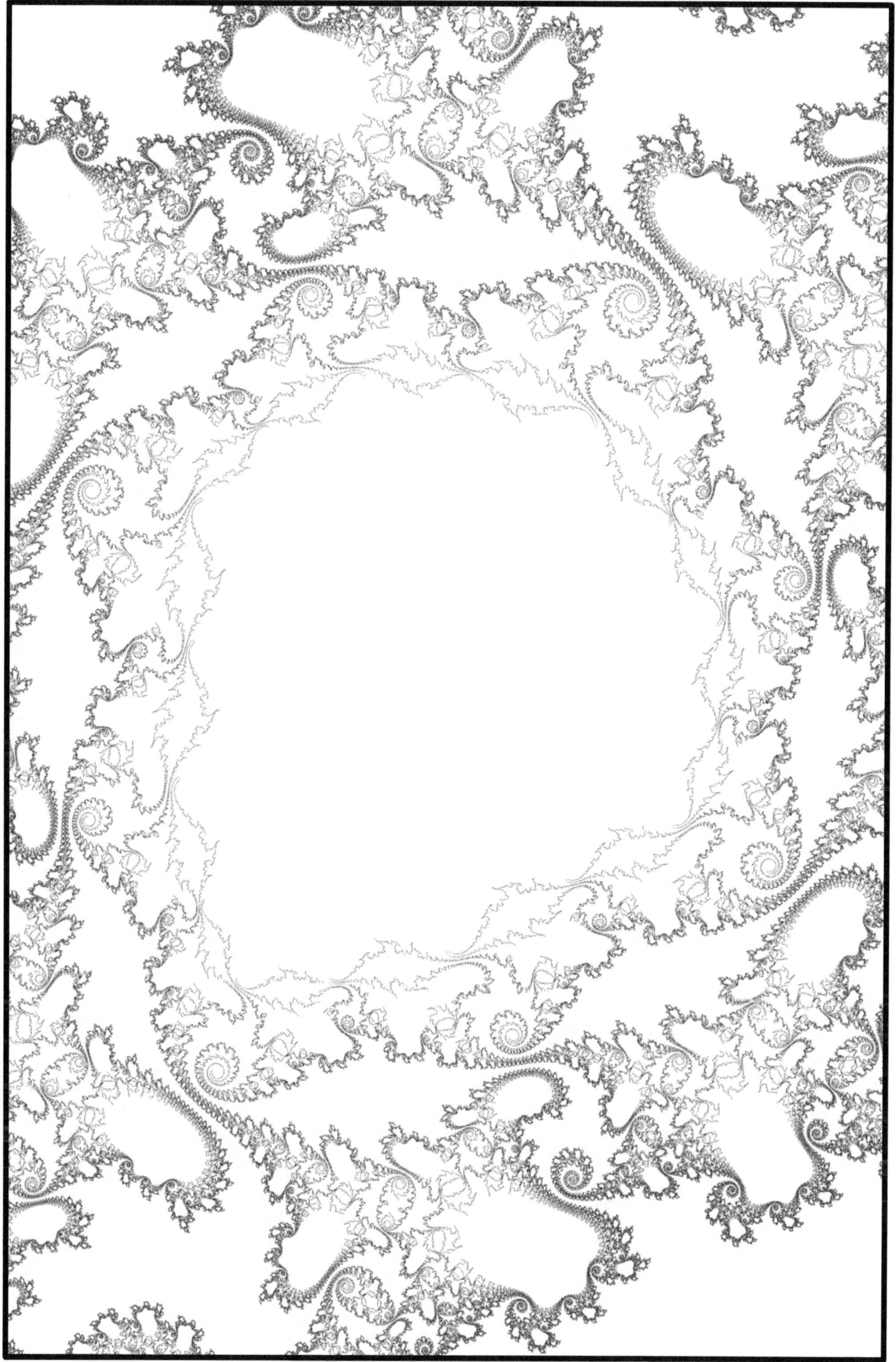

Mirror Mirror

Zoom: 0.000002286284052546537,0.000001434616154297156
Location: 0.25952865176548007,-0.4906791972648593
Iterations: 912

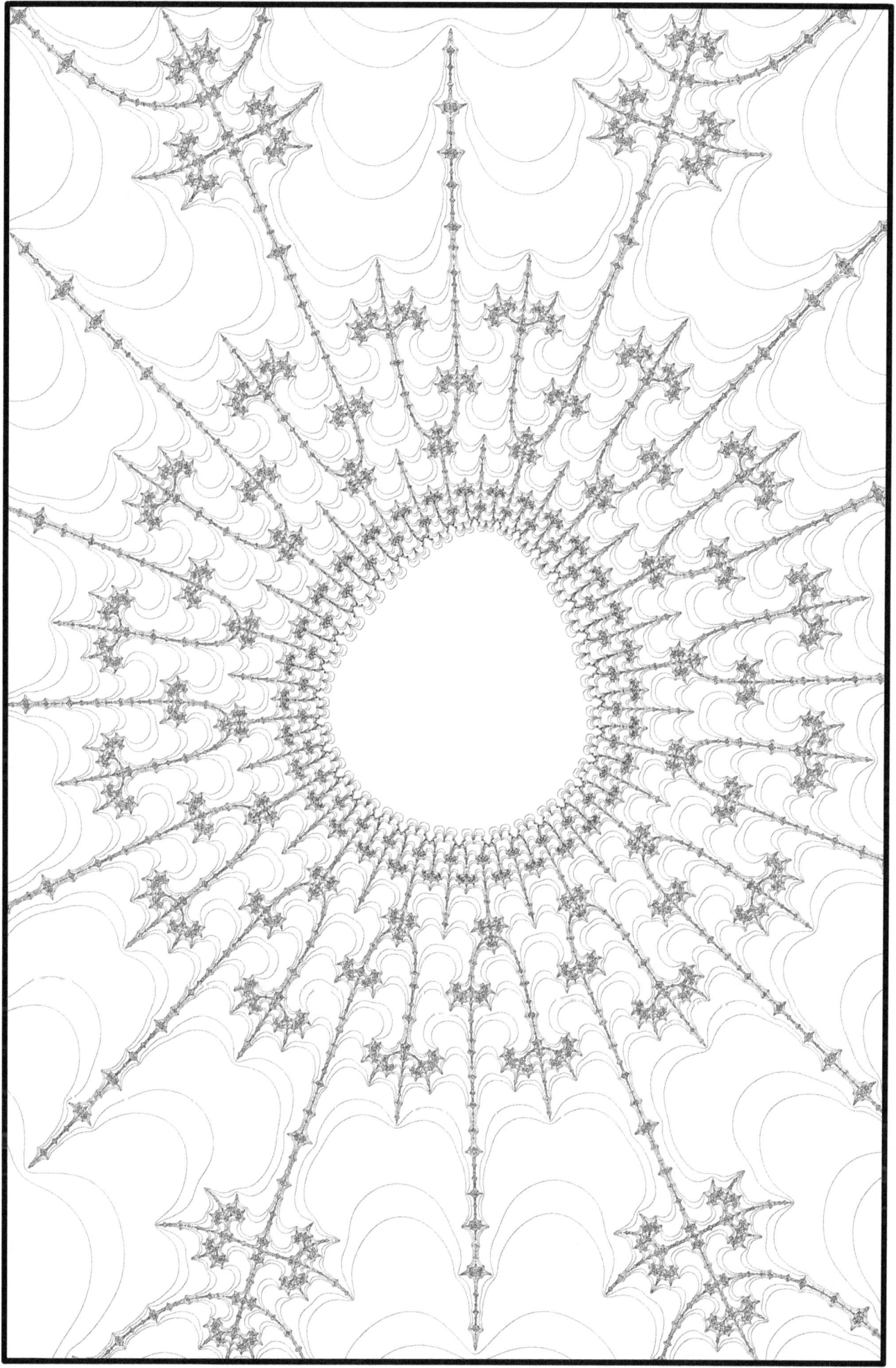

Nobs 4

Zoom: 3.663662139746433e-11,2.2988986497280265e-11
Location: -1.7400326789931033,0.000013742122438754124
Iterations: 185

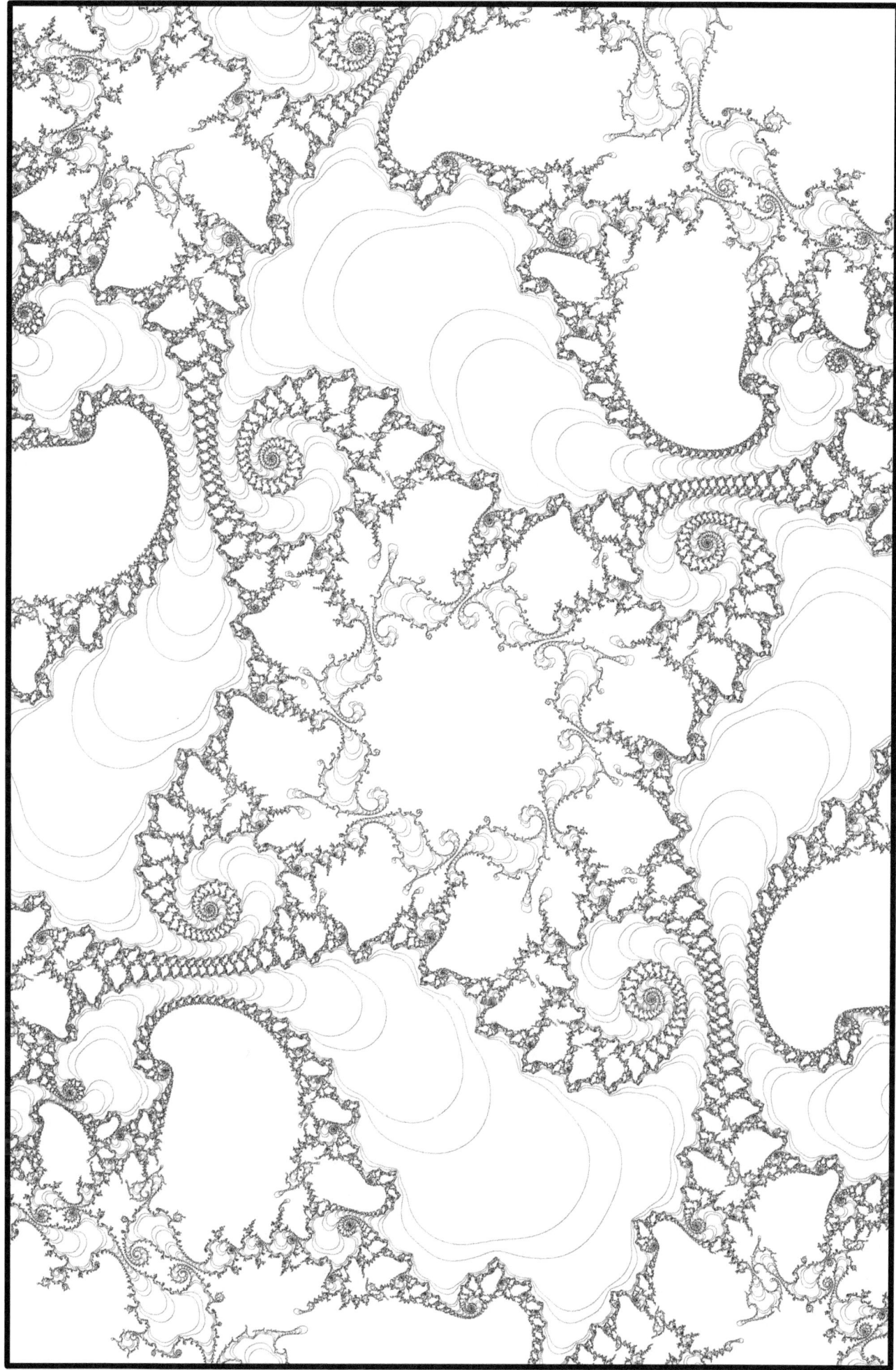

Dark Magic

Zoom: 1.102482091147894e-7,5.496268697450338e-8
Location: -0.7464262685931518,0.07024519209768057
Iterations: 1105

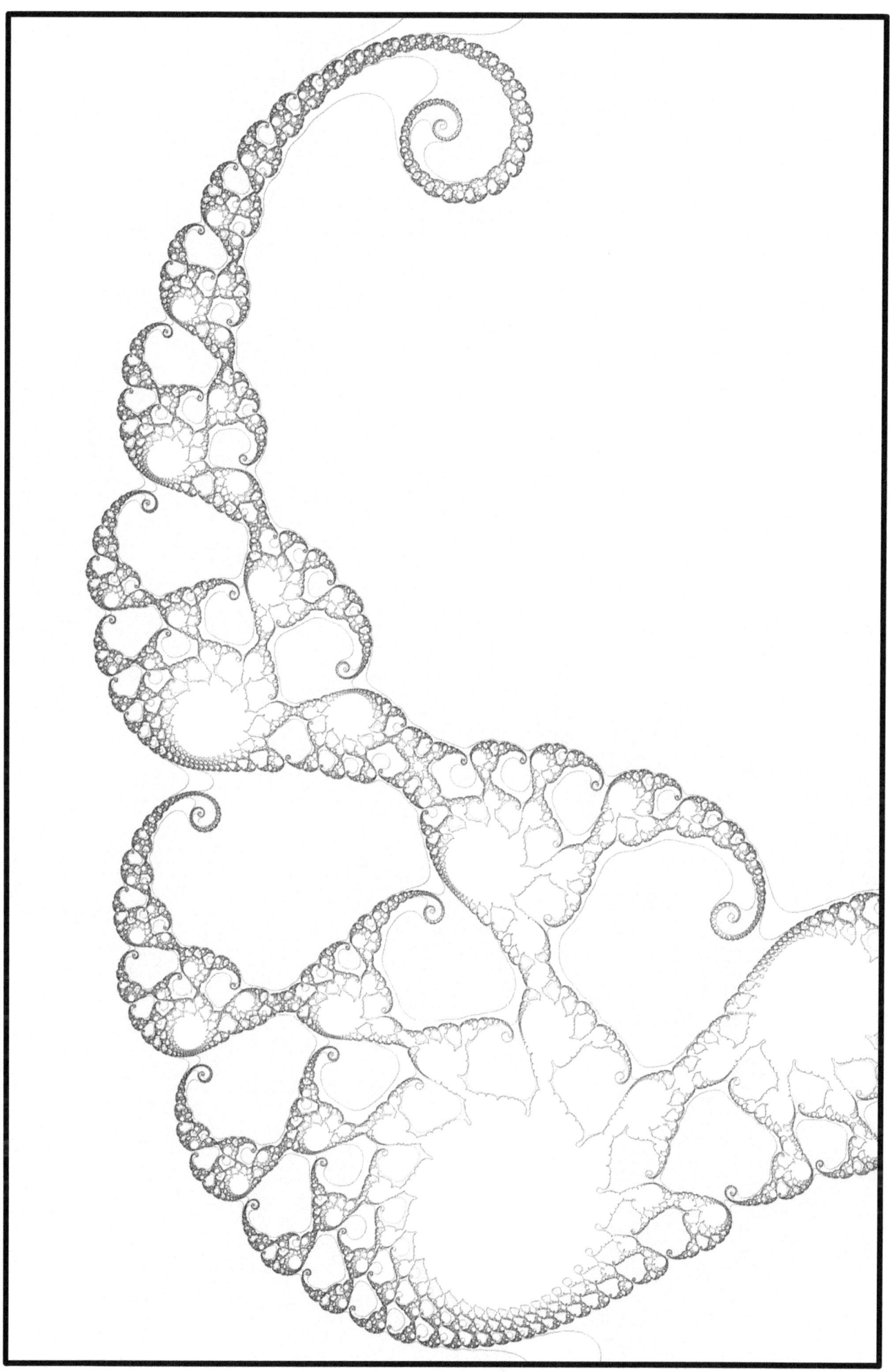

Big Foot

Zoom: 0.00011356418763834193,0.00006547628981046664
Location: 0.2681065042581083,0.003653467887613132
Iterations: 118

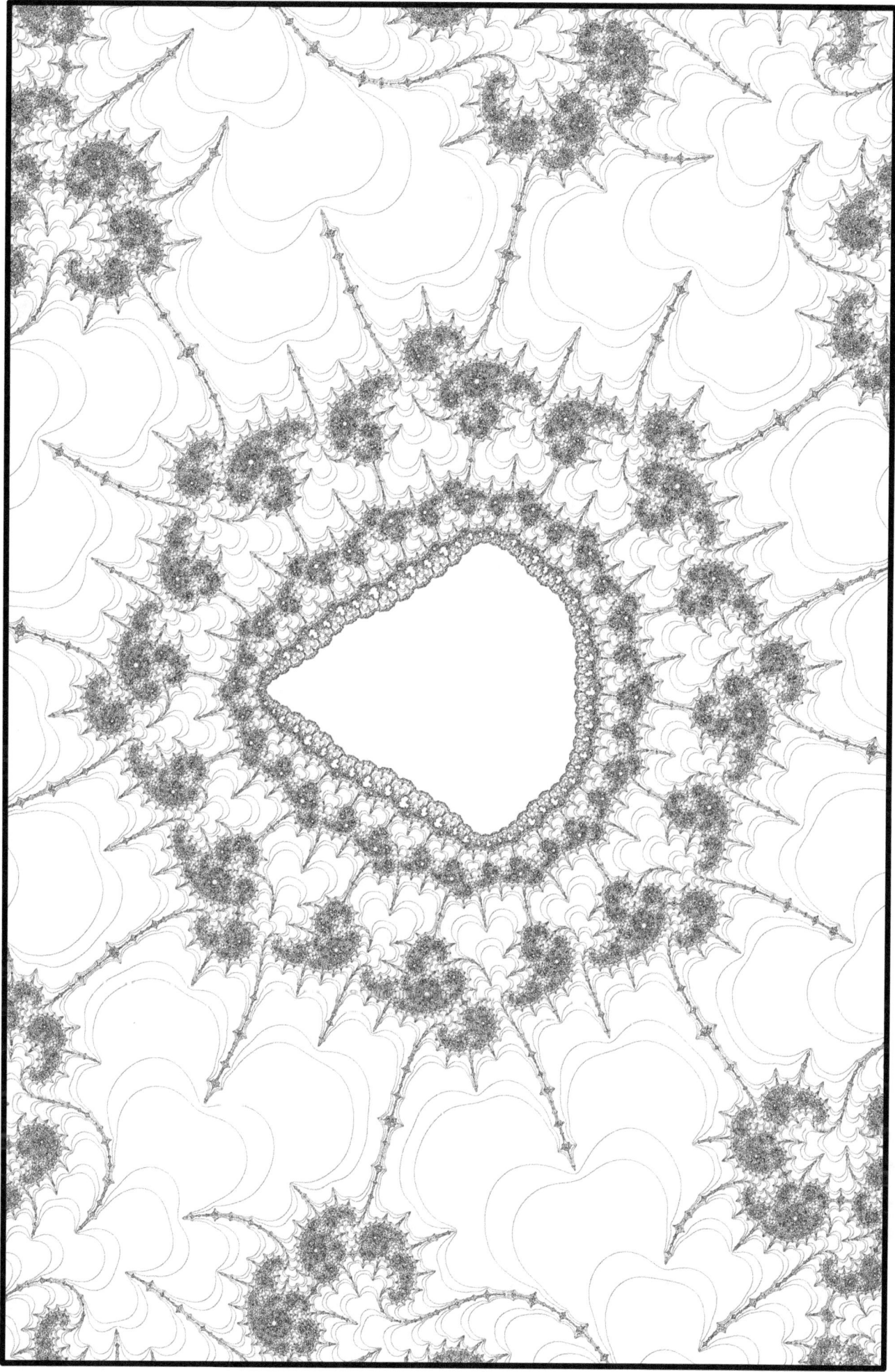

Shamrock Horse

Zoom: 6.614909585899829e-9,4.1507773899156124e-9
Location: -1.7476679611060701,0.0014813576631526482
Iterations: 281

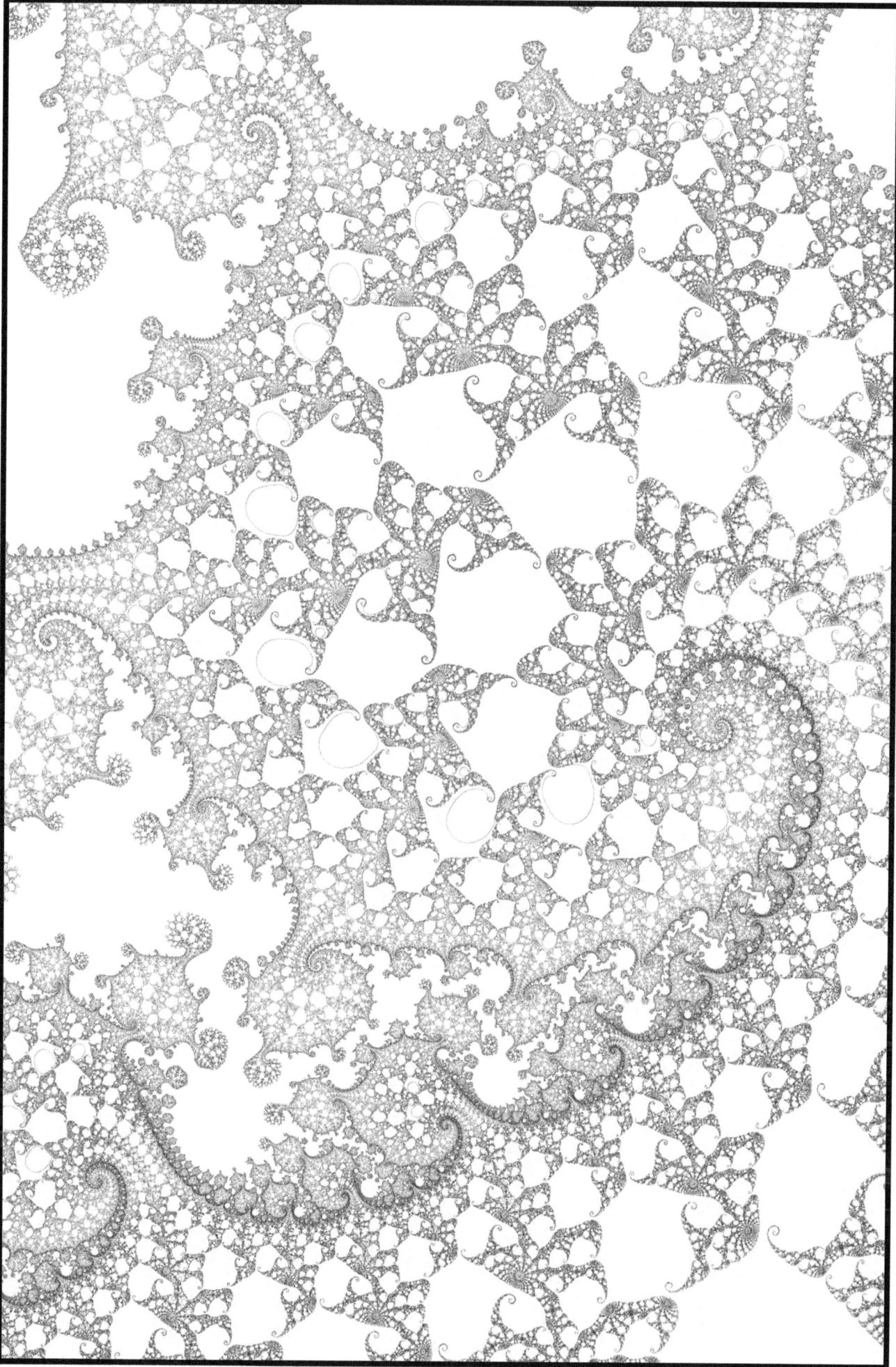

Cave Of Wonder

Zoom: 1.9360363445570402e-8,9.651835657605859e-9
Location: 0.2717332981931142,0.00489358310993337
Iterations: 5592

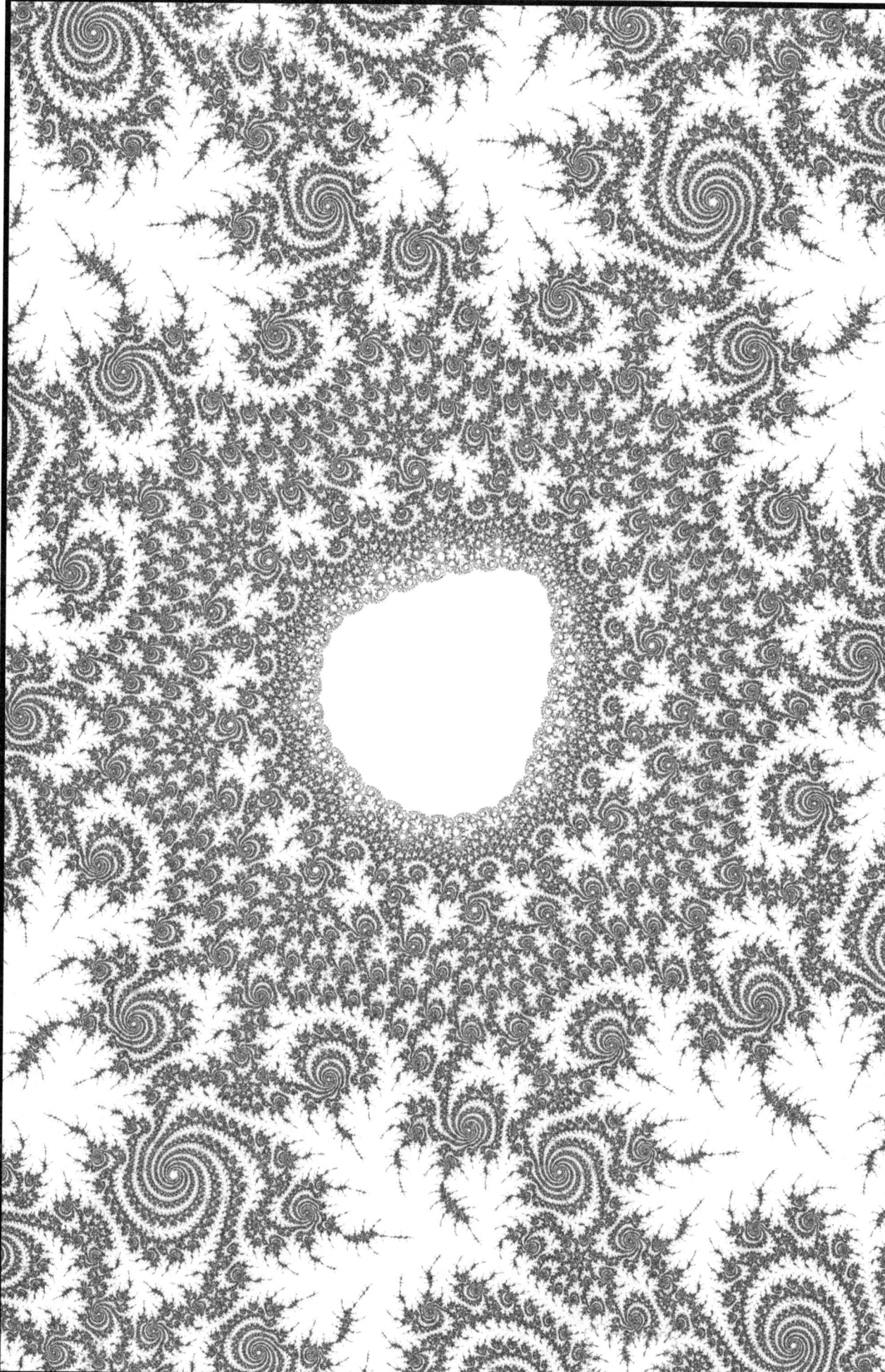

Galaxy Set

Zoom: 7.497432888860765e-10,4.704549944819234e-10
Location: -1.3593662522381058,0.03191034824271469
Iterations: 3096

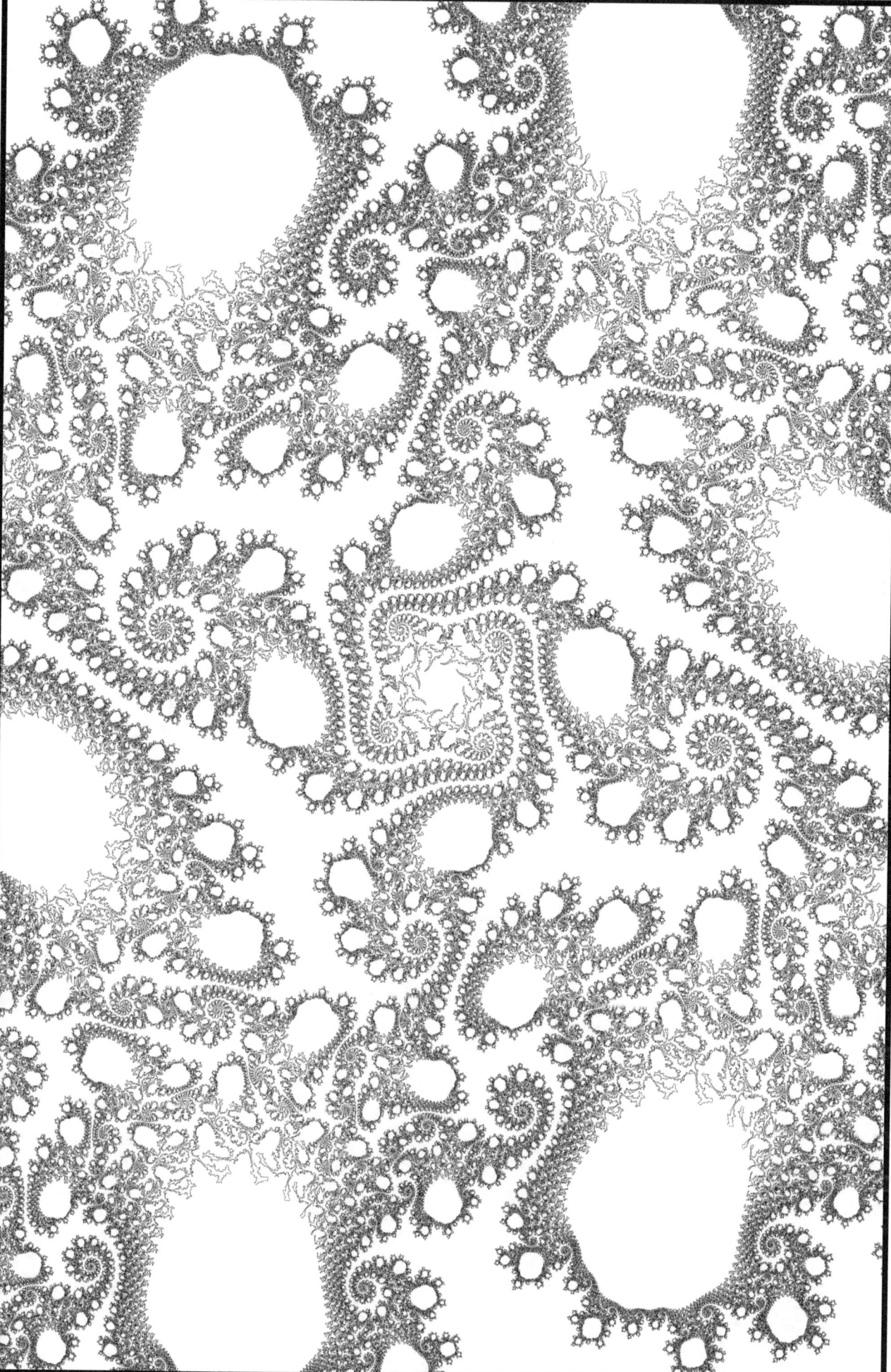

Spindly Spiral Square

Zoom: 2.5285620746648777e-9,1.5866427425692182e-9
Location: -0.3470821726004512,0.6064884447423726
Iterations: 1335

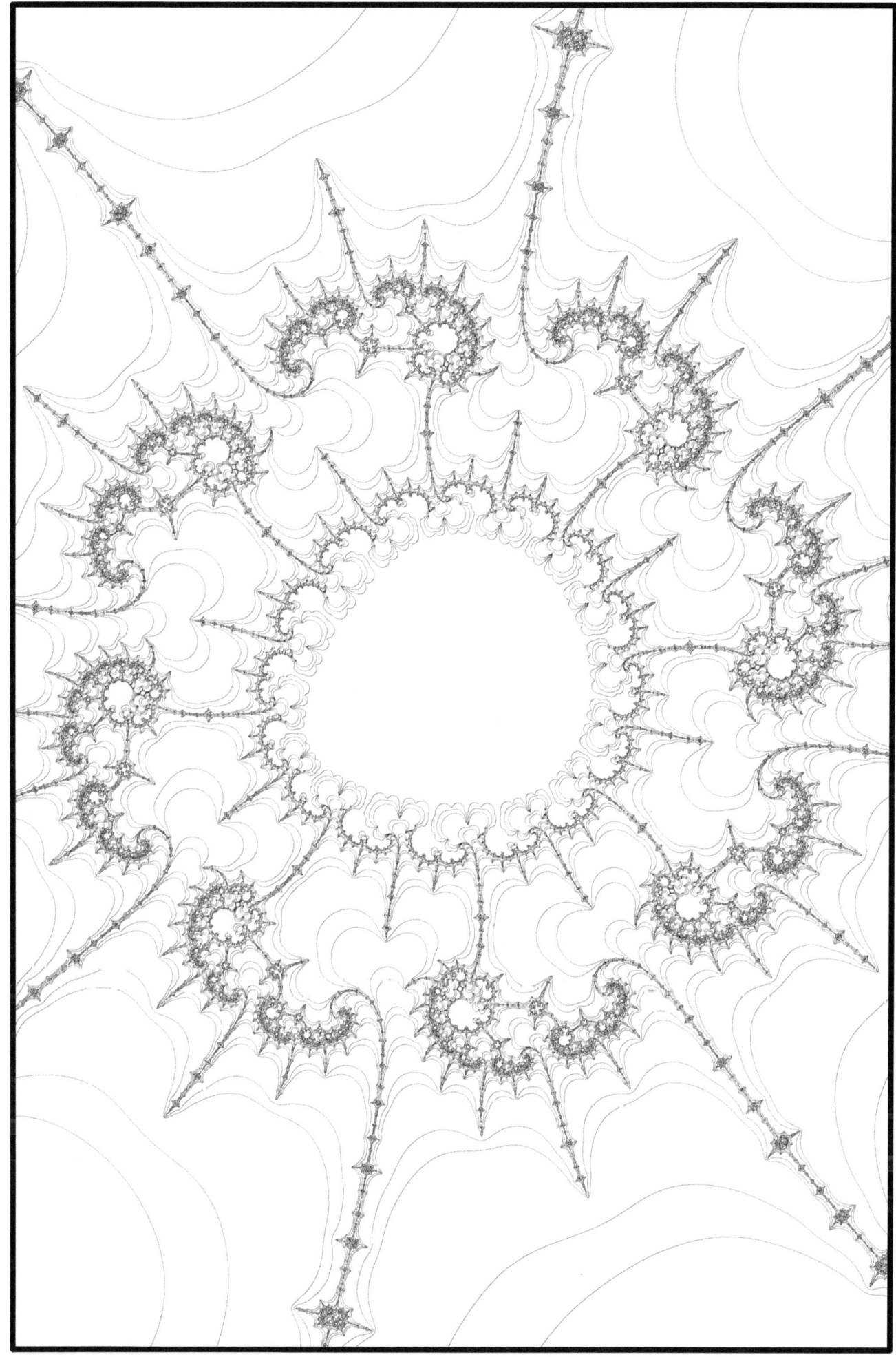

Nobs 6

Zoom: 7.328088166856449e-7,4.5982884977882537e-7
Location: -1.7471072116773418,-0.0013777645836535045
Iterations: 137

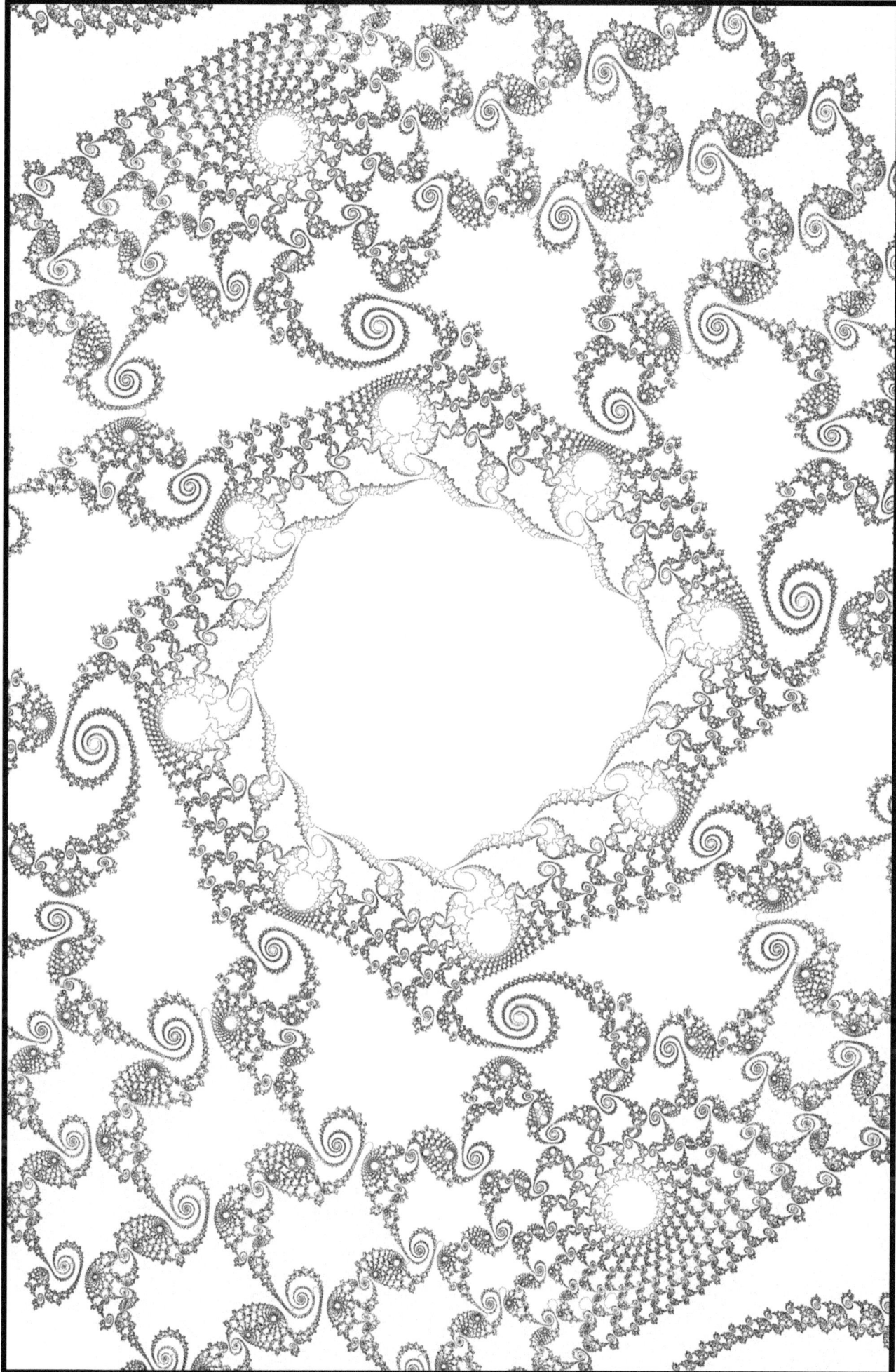

White Crabs

Zoom: 0.00000349506835369644,0.0000017424169464621368
Location: -0.7602771149524642,-0.08453465440374948
Iterations: 570

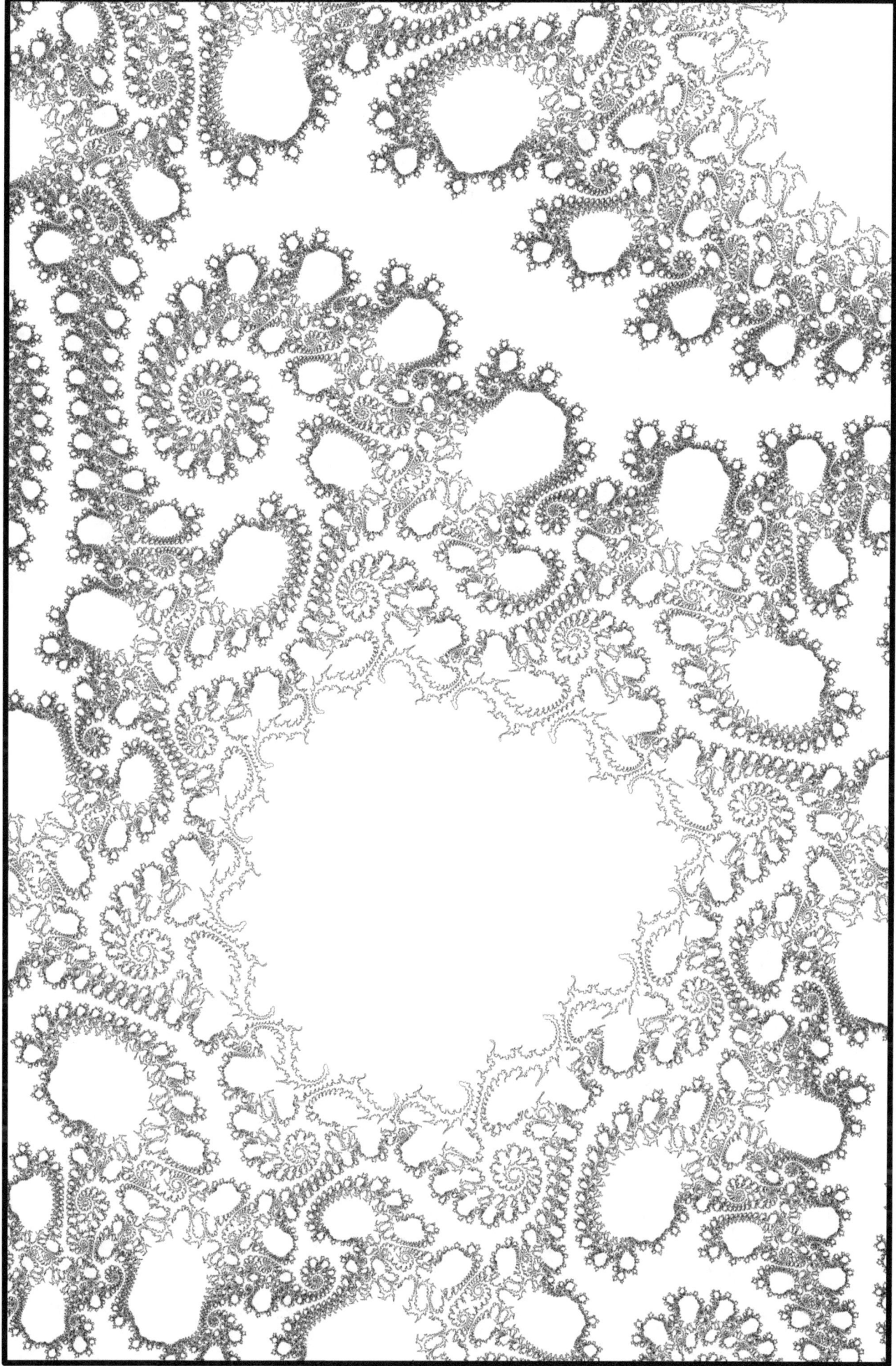

Spindly Spiral

Zoom: 0.0000018797765044059,0.0000011795374842472336
Location: -0.347101003693252,0.6065032301522607
Iterations: 1035

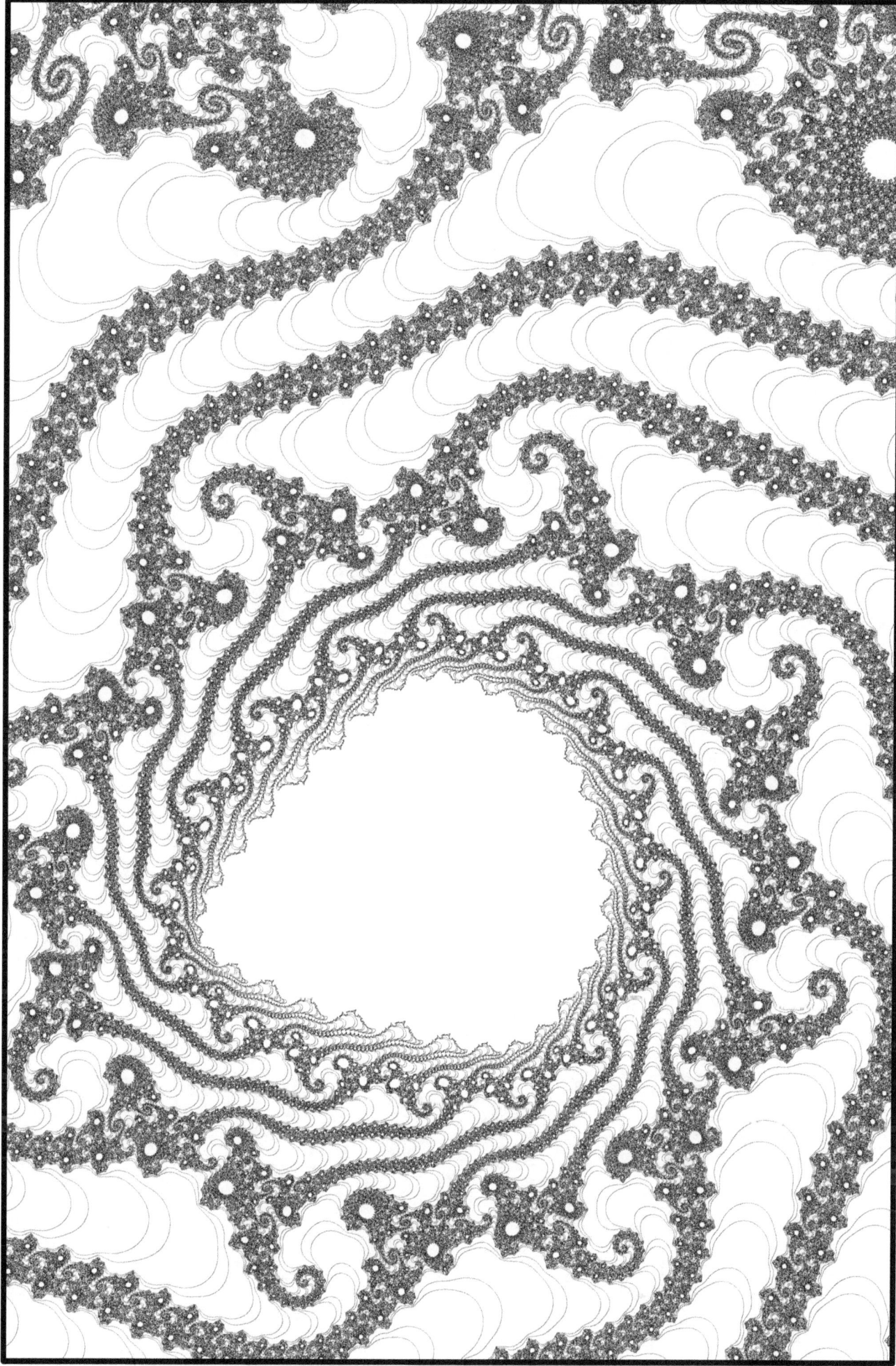

Stripeset 2

Zoom: 3.9913344932315446e-8,2.504515103781498e-8
Location: -0.7443556304909813,0.12121279169815033
Iterations: 600

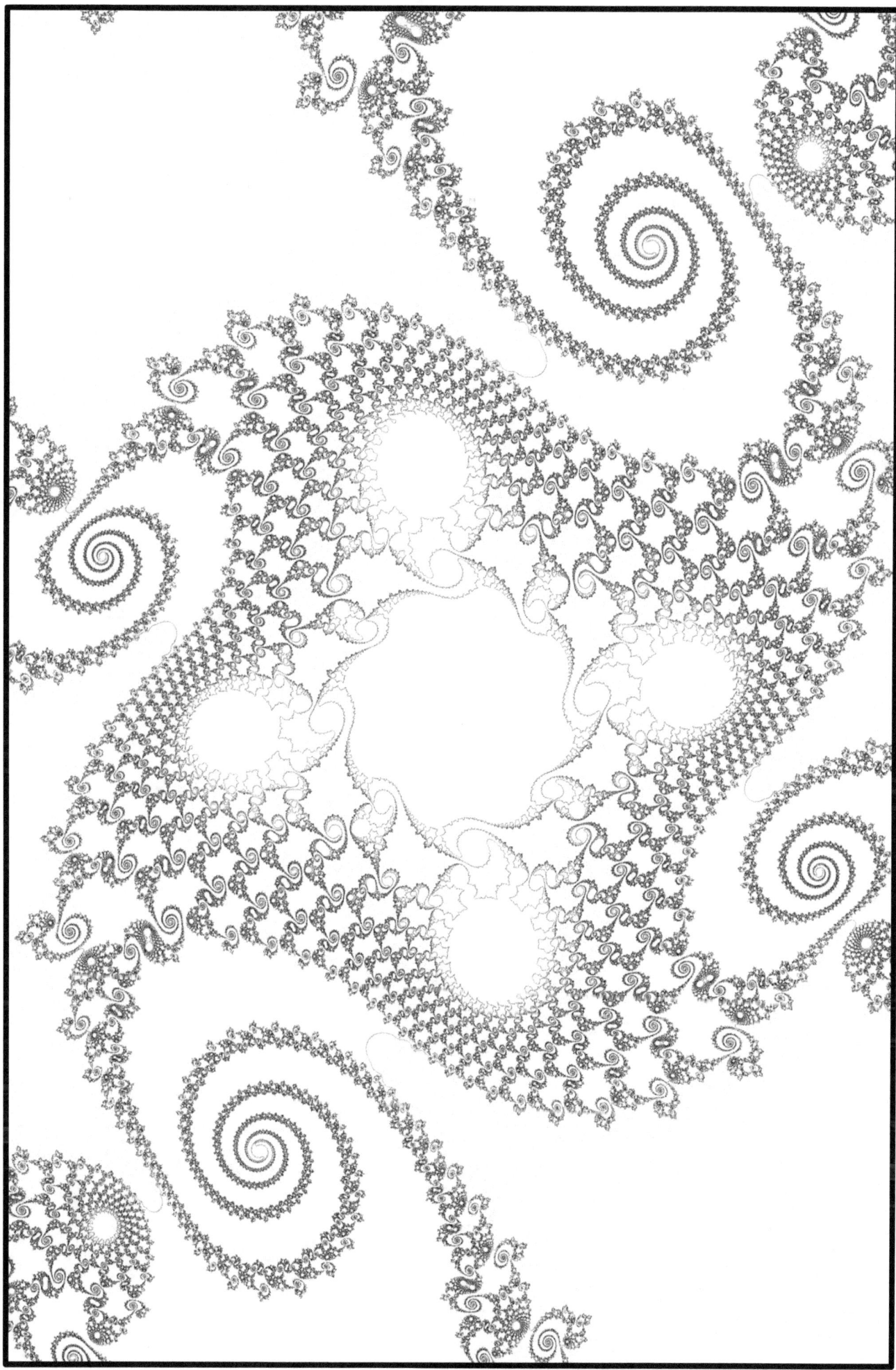

Four Crab Star

Zoom: 0.000001692551578207951,8.437976755404916e-7
Location: -0.7604569778846669,-0.08467442926039923
Iterations: 626

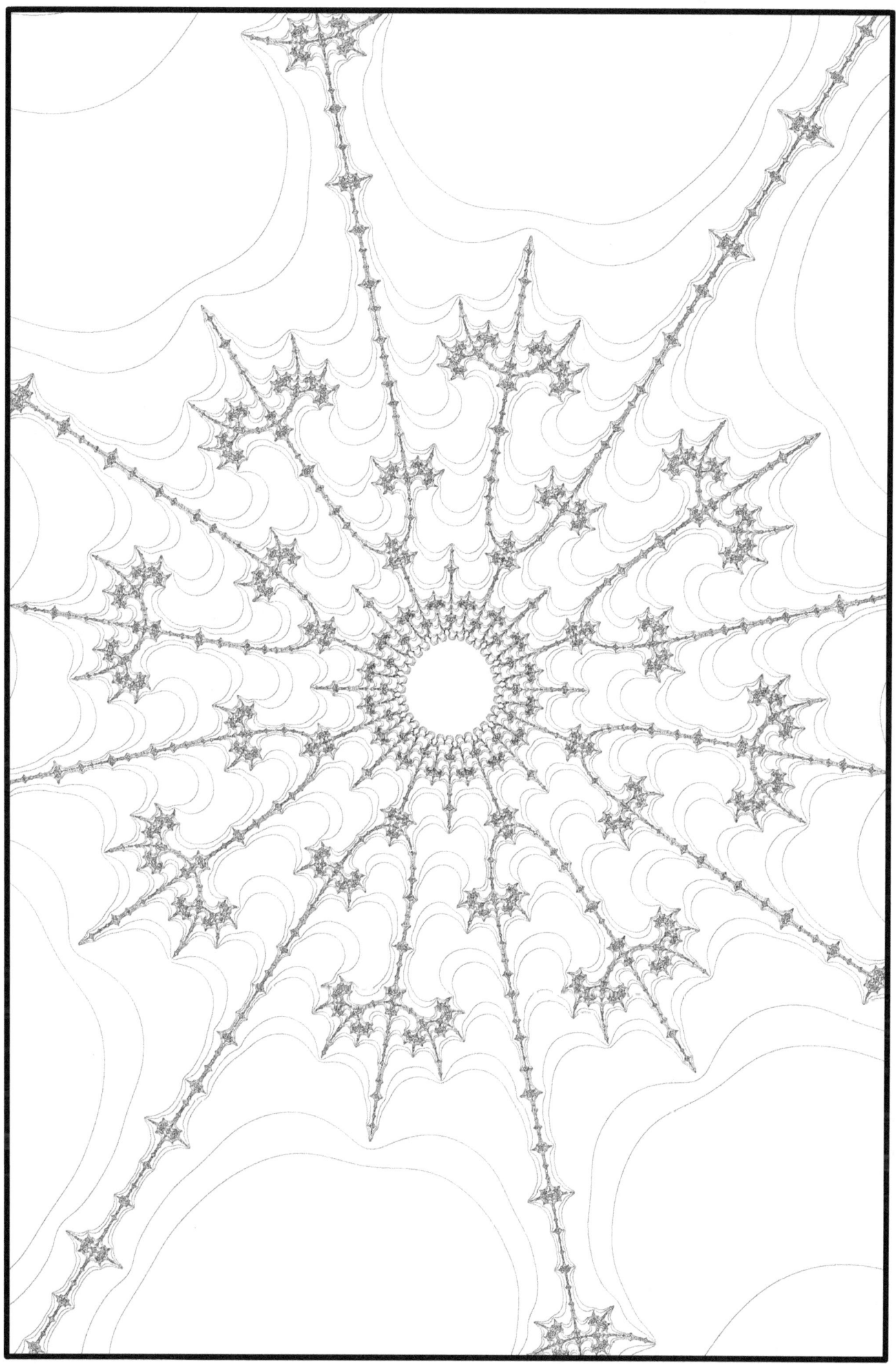

Nobs 5

Zoom: 1.8114680862112034e-10,1.1366742725832875e-10
Location: -1.740032955886183,0.000016553380890648658
Iterations: 150

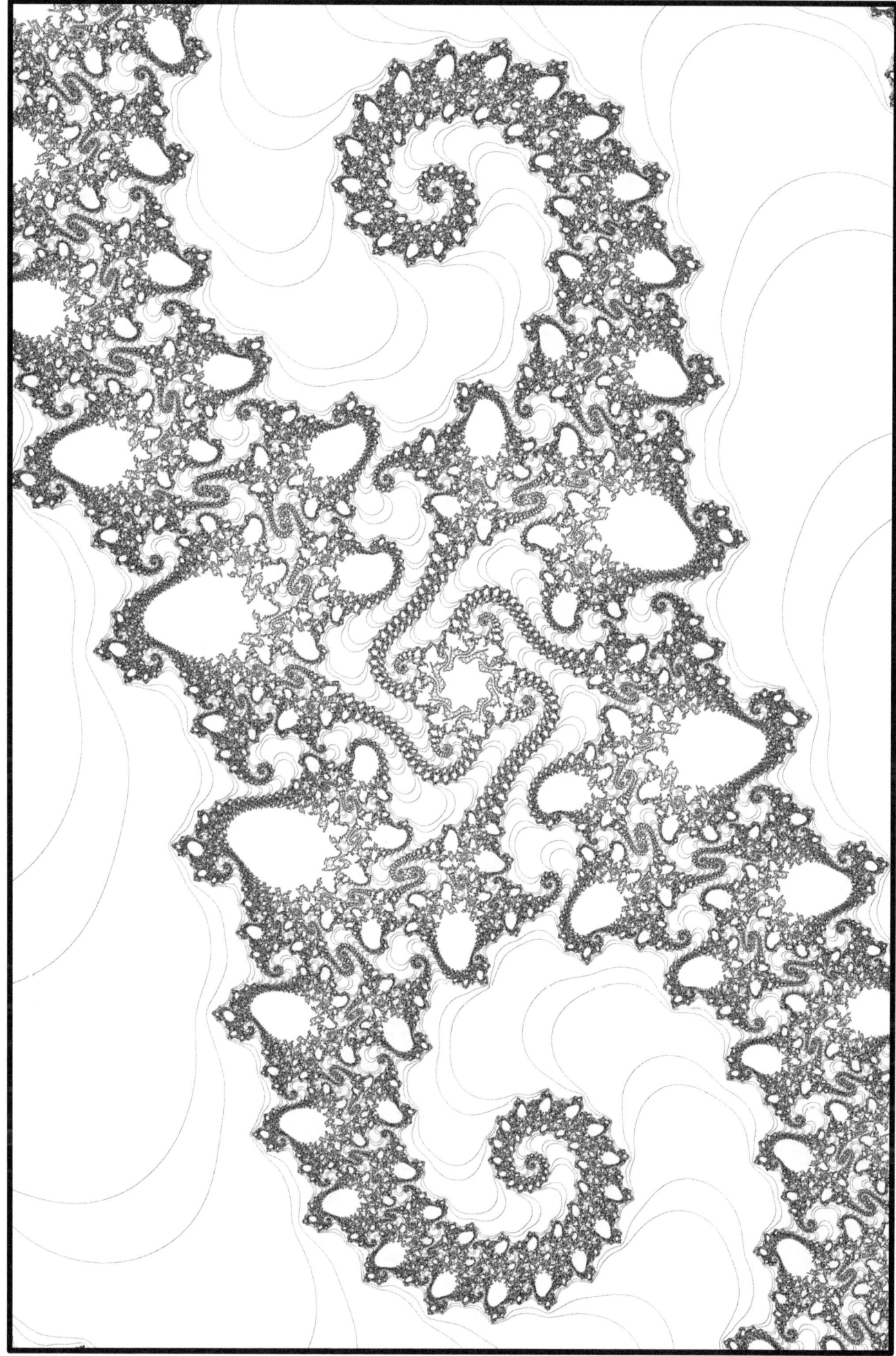

Tails Entwine 2

Zoom: 0.000001907536368437066,0.00000119695647007921152
Location: -0.7424945117983701,0.11087017982661125
Iterations: 421

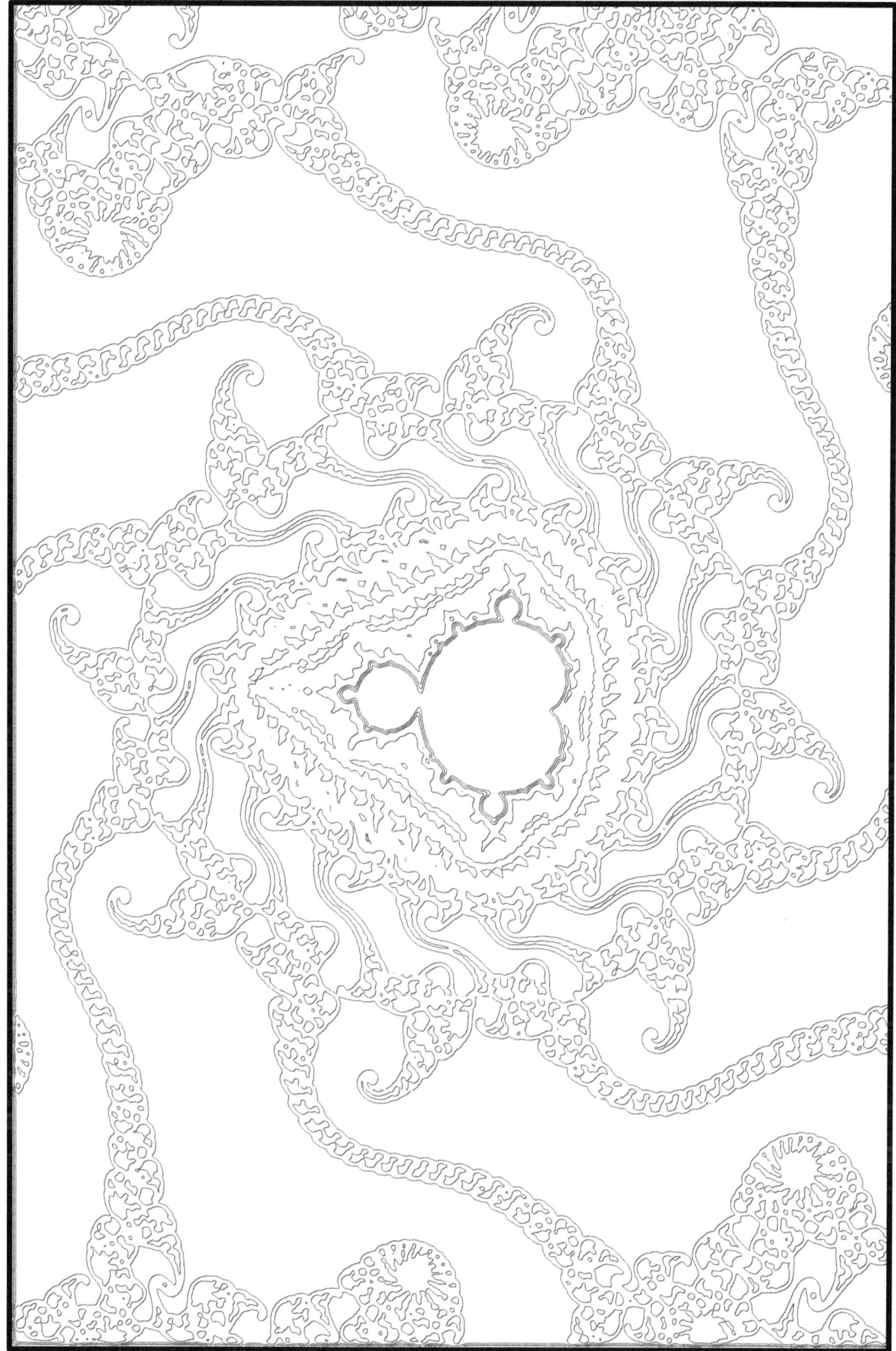

Greyscale

Zoom: 3.331200140107967e-8,2.0902886195707623e-8
Location: 0.28724876453064546,0.012997881783608303
Iterations: 5970

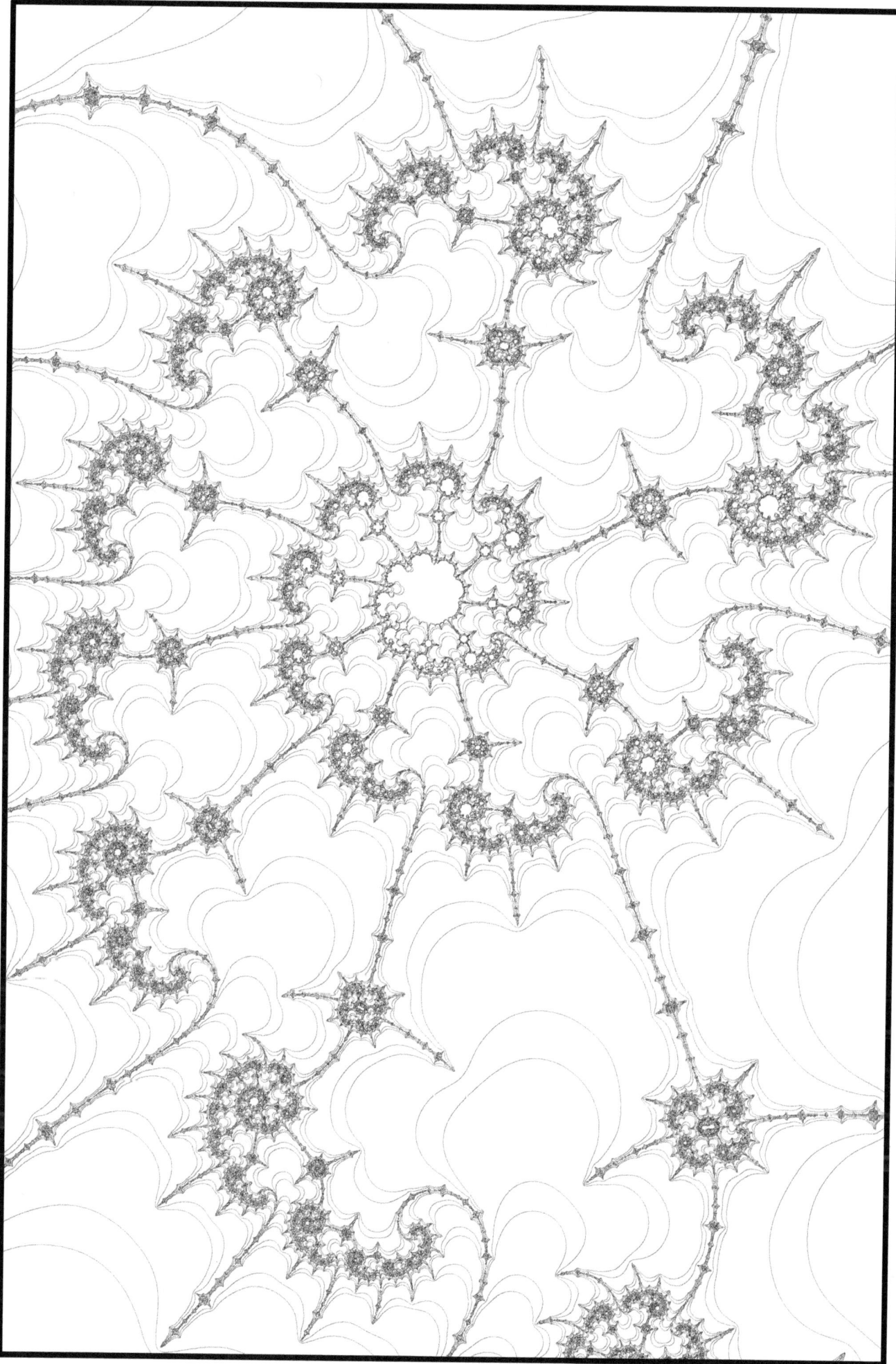

Nobs 7

Zoom: 2.121241367995996e-8,1.3310538248713299e-8
Location: -1.7471073962523995,-0.0013778674951005893
Iterations: 177

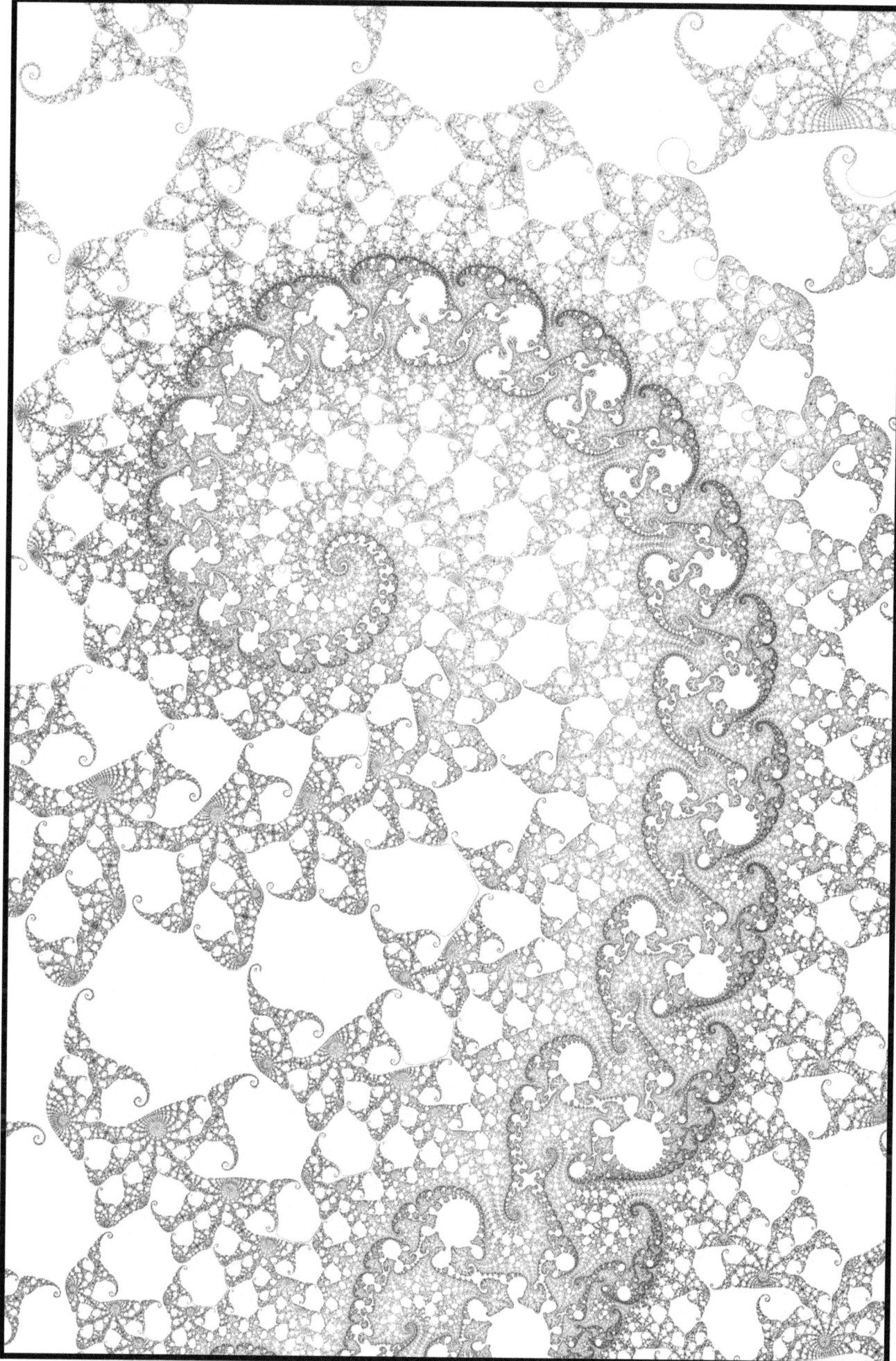

Cave Of Wonder 2

Zoom: 4.474525086362948e-9,2.807711472944949e-9
Location: 0.27173329721545714,0.004893587512924419
Iterations: 1976

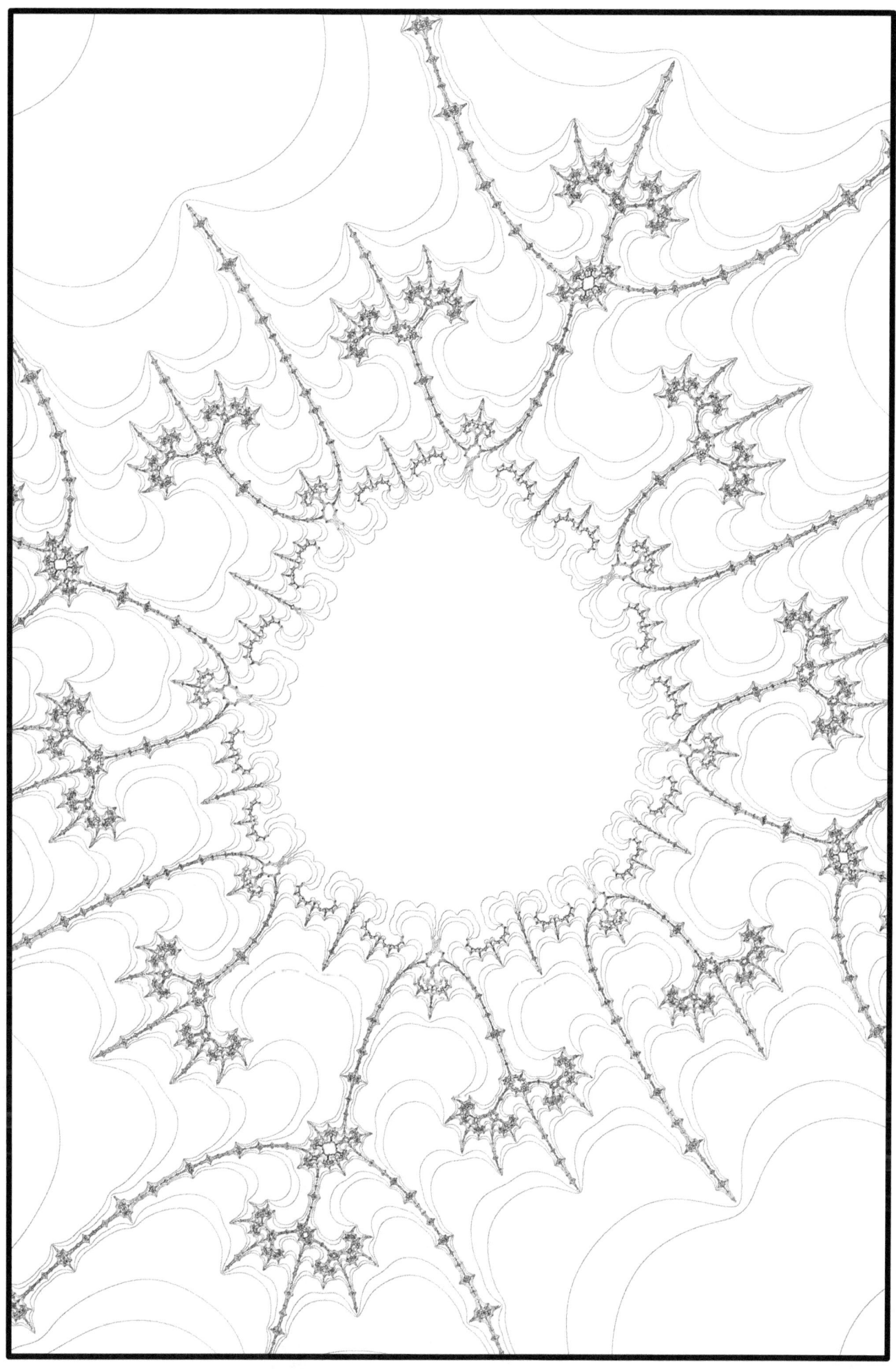

Asym Spike Nobs

Zoom: 0.000016410304083101103,0.0000102972713773306516
Location: -1.7397134338329994,0.00019855678080589763
Iterations: 89

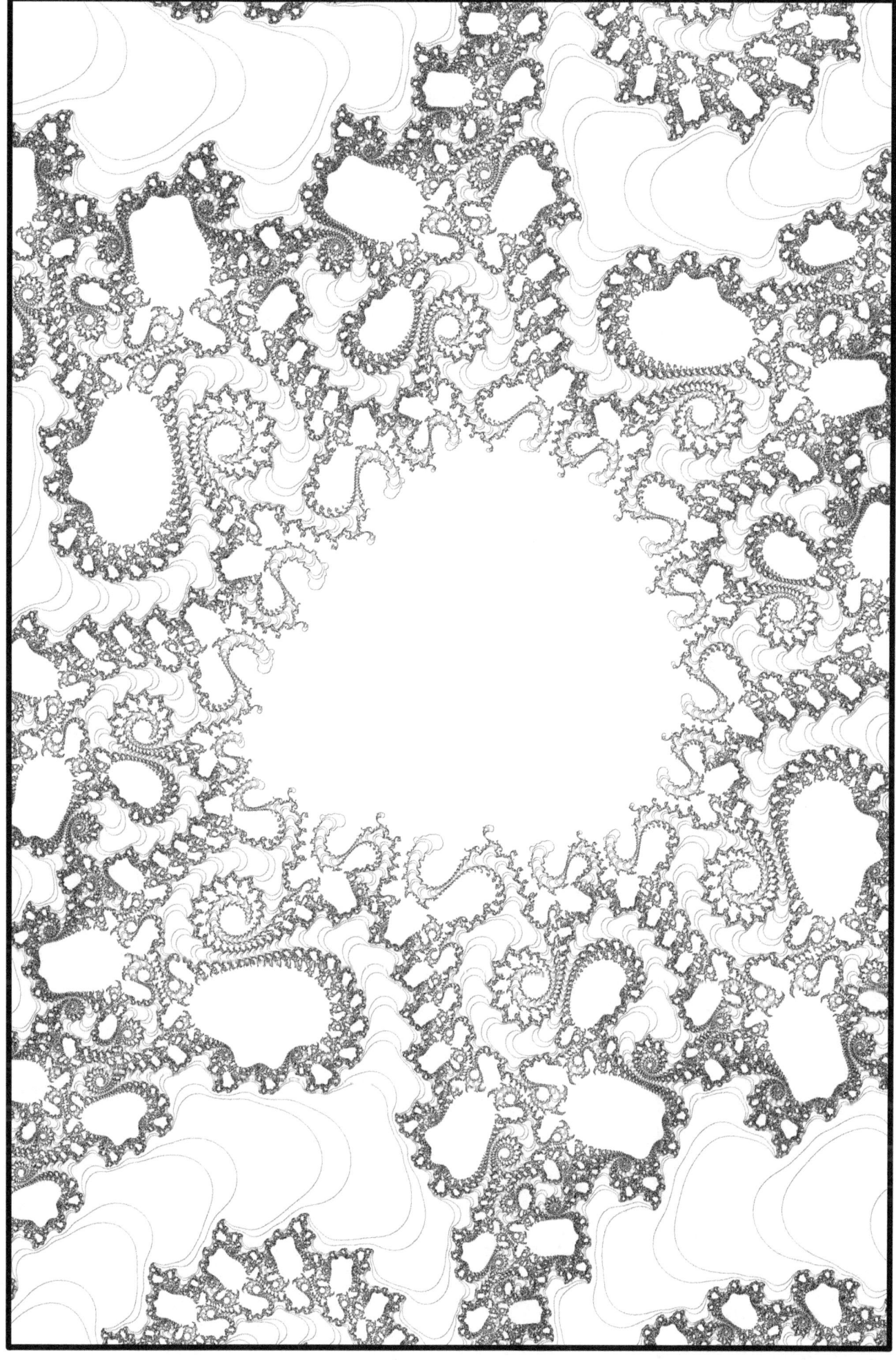

Colorbook 4

Zoom: 0.00000155608774387298 8,9.764266222213487e-7
Location: 0.24045005030634498,0.5099444643877931
Iterations: 600

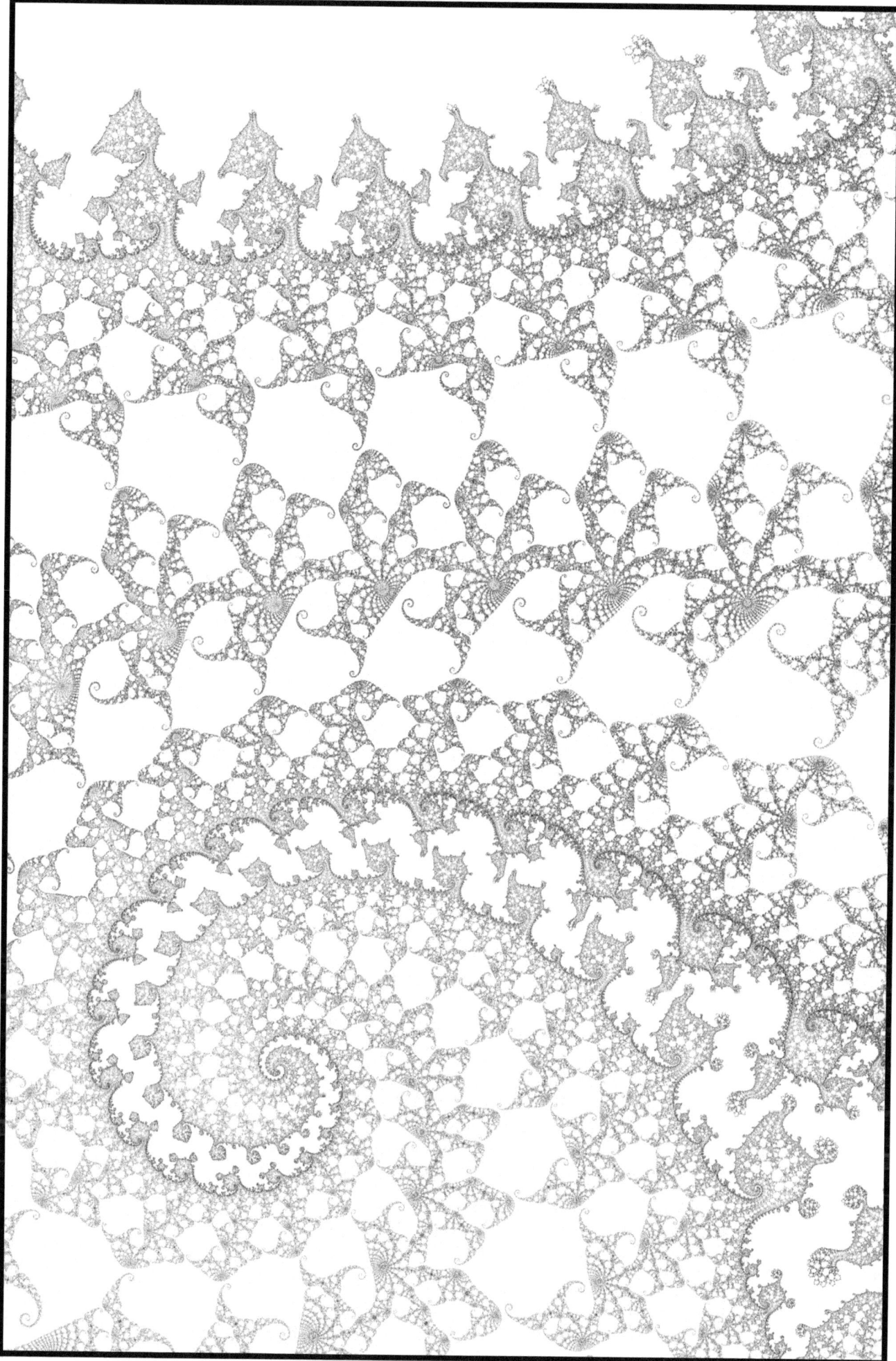

Cave Of Wonder 3

Zoom: 1.954579035572084e-9,1.2264751849707849e-9
Location: 0.27173329935161616,0.0048935775085227635
Iterations: 2276

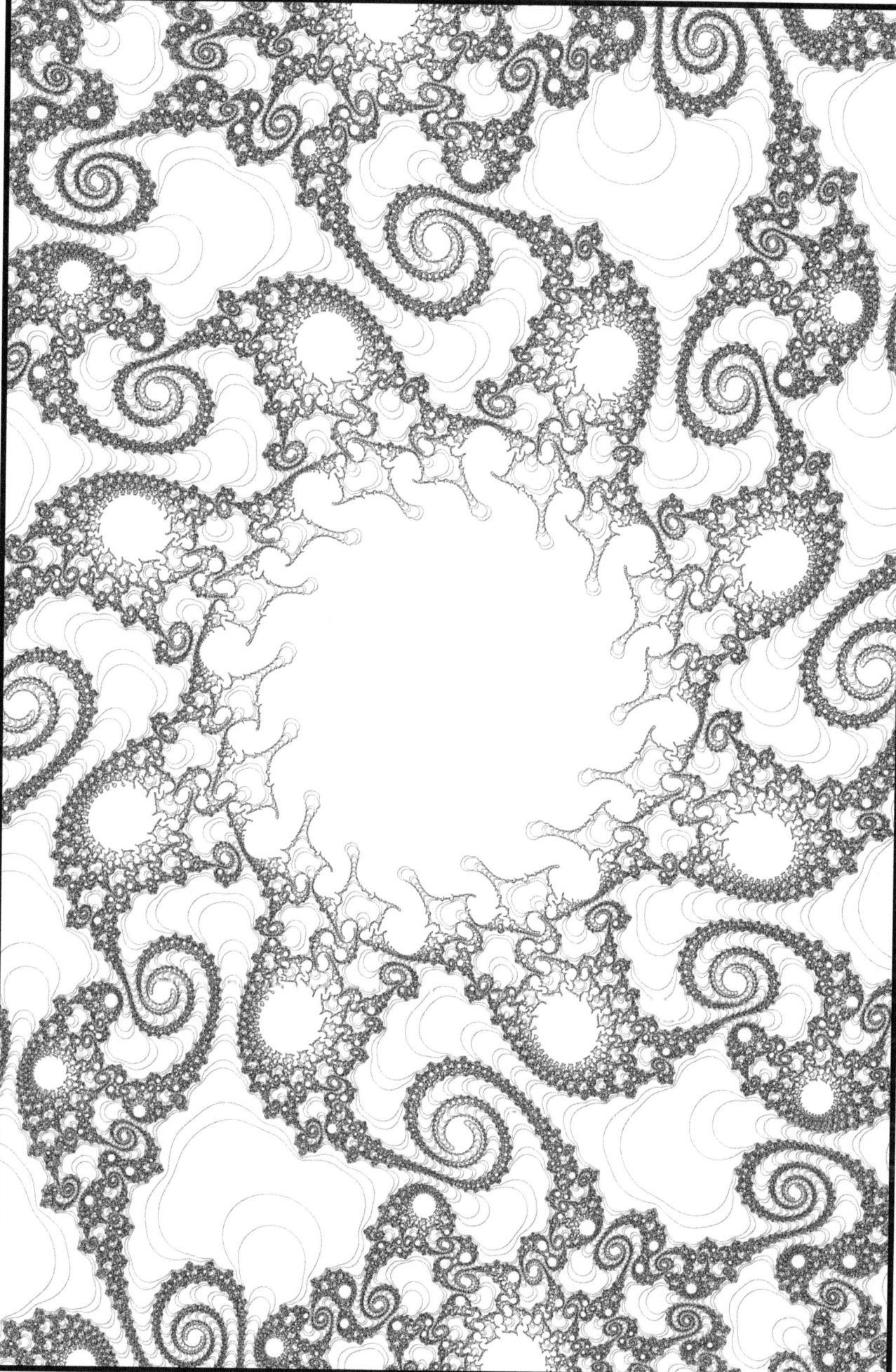

One Crab

Zoom: 5.062999621810812e-8,3.176972275276007e-8
Location: -0.760558722039757,-0.08474025297489492
Iterations: 489

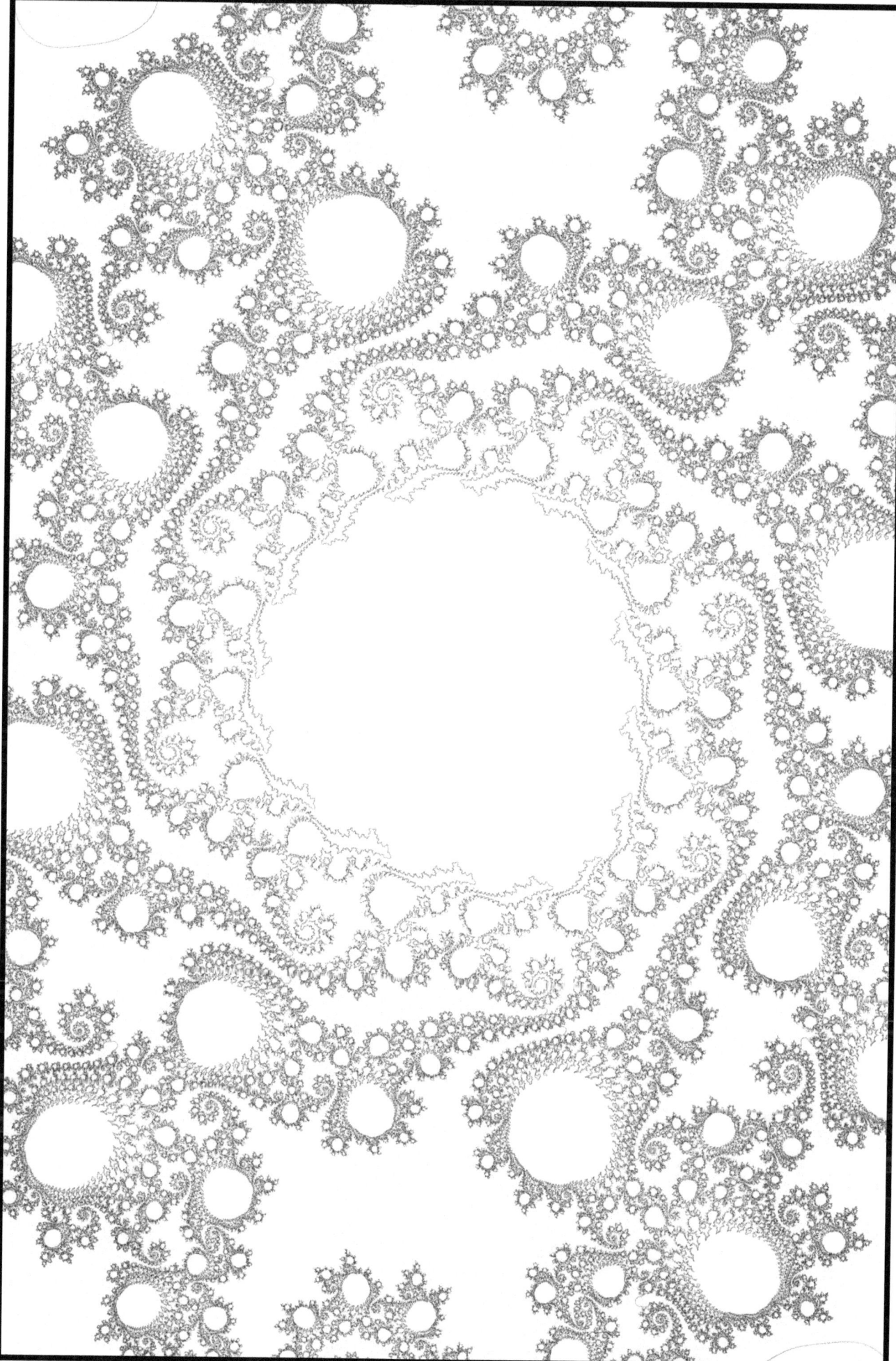

Smoke And Mirrors

Zoom: 1.0070438224400451e-7,6.319080665310487e-8
Location: 0.1059709444412161,-0.6007237503329497
Iterations: 850

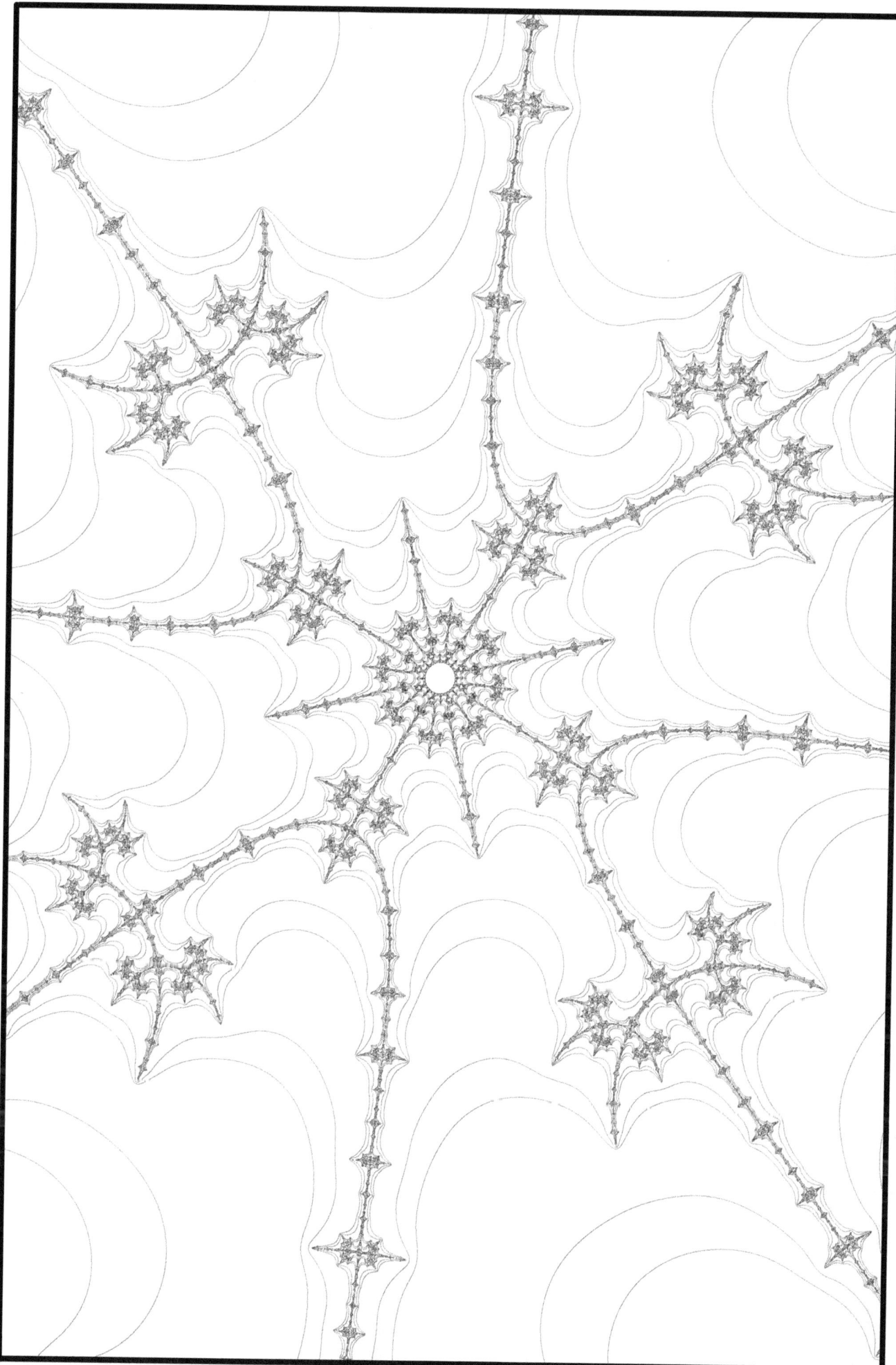

Nobs 2

Zoom: 9.219490033588595e-10,5.785119378991728e-10
Location: -1.7400326789995473,0.000013742131378076901
Iterations: 130

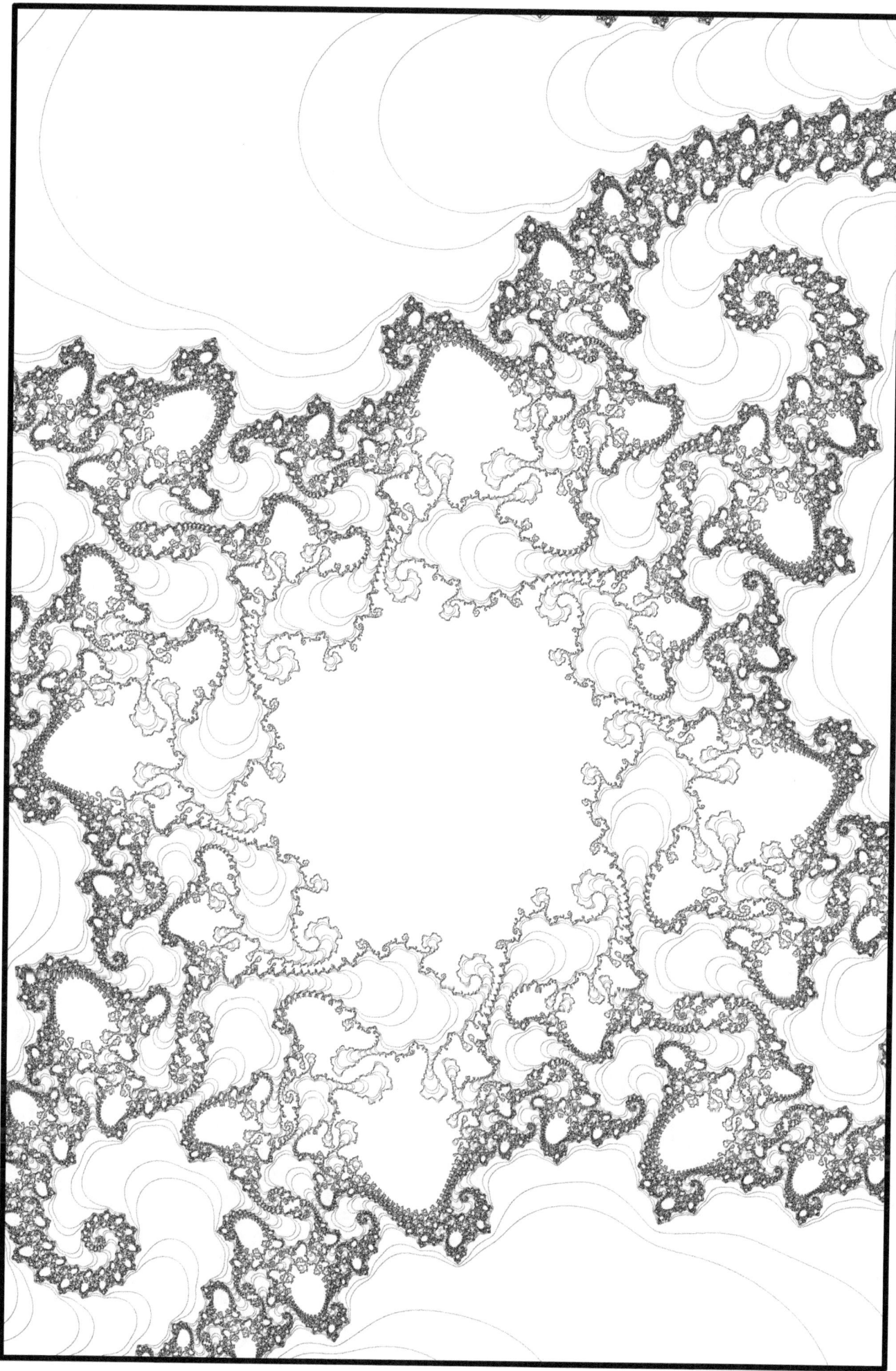

Stripeset 1

Zoom: 0.00000288090632307789,0.0000018077345837692021
Location: -0.7438404626996045,0.12138416249009114
Iterations: 320

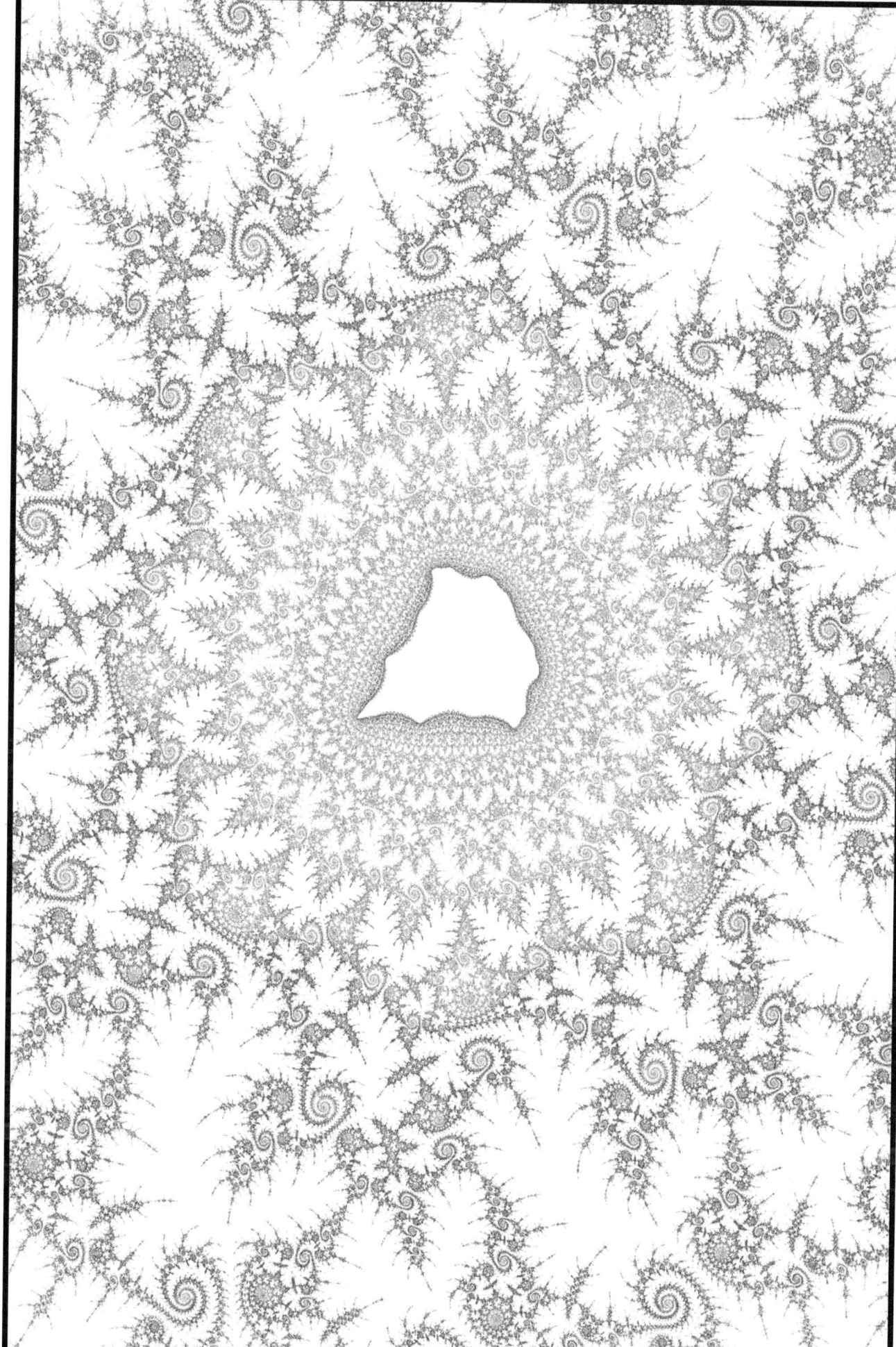

Inside Prickle 3

Zoom: 4.61501104004013e-12,2.3007485494887546e-12
Location: -1.3691652371759793,-0.006555815741688641
Iterations: 3747

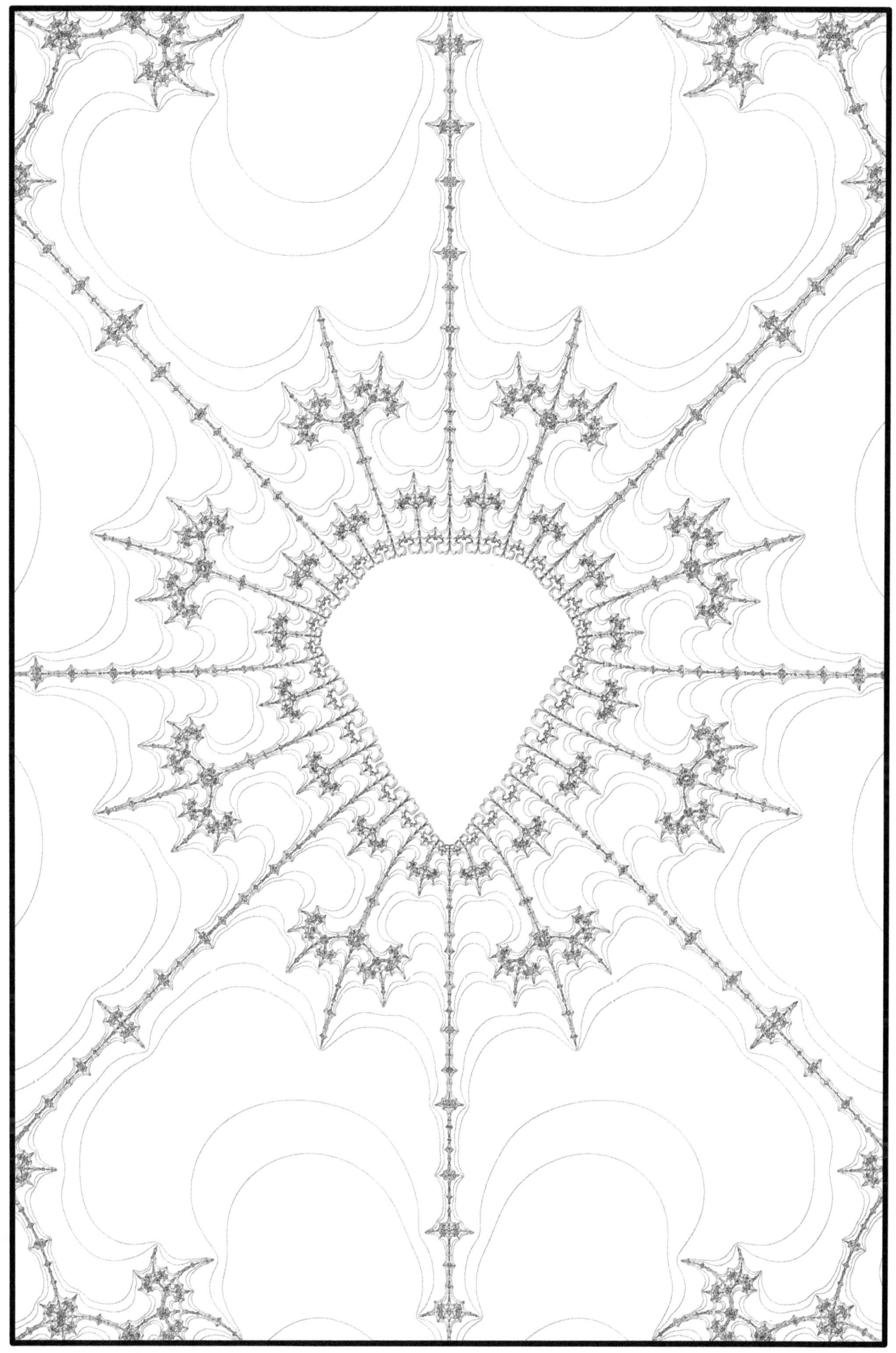

Spike Nobs

Zoom: 0.00006194368112535515,0.0000388689259763009
Location: -1.7397201493774237,7.353408149064604e-8
Iterations: 91

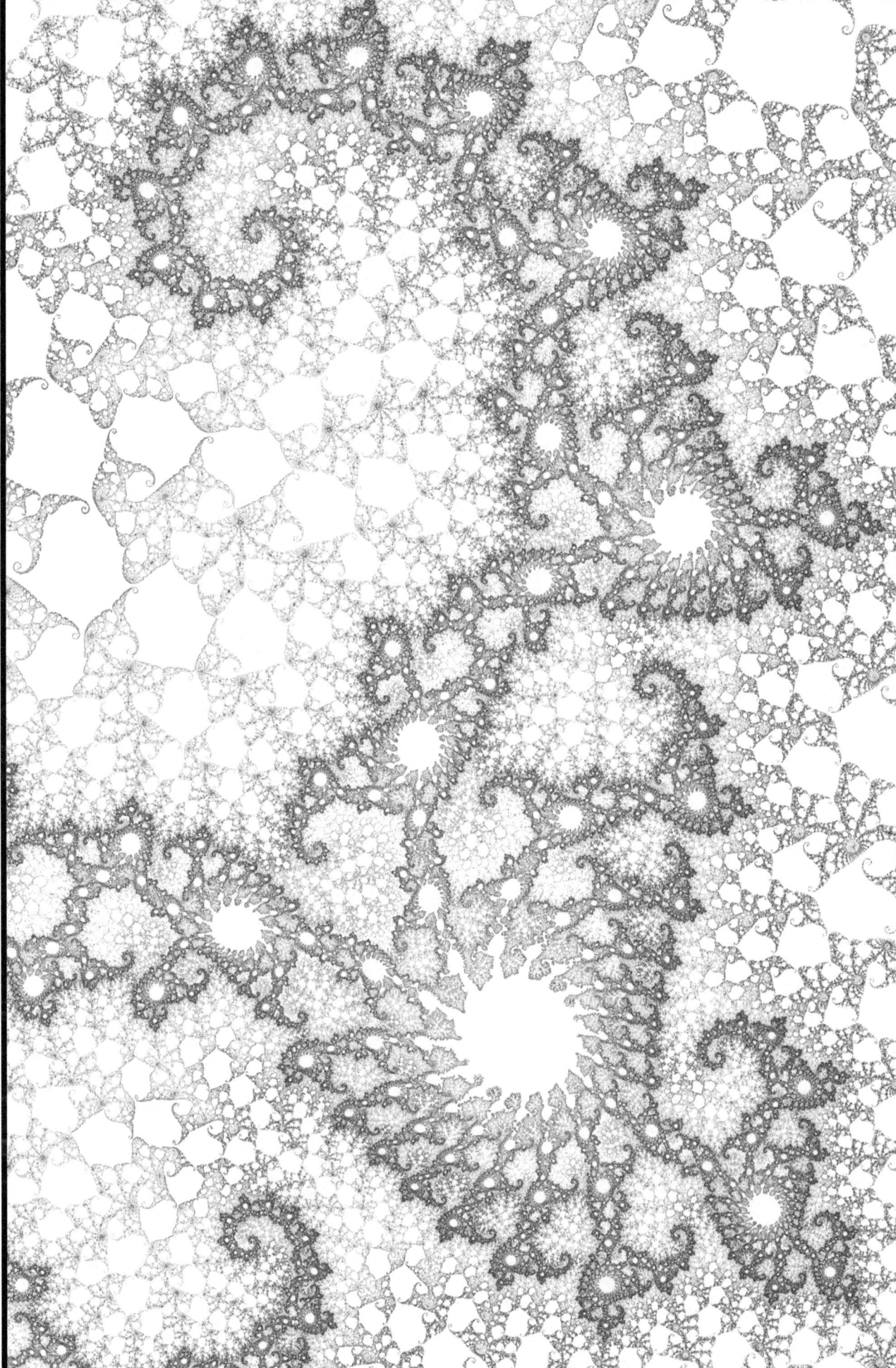

Bubble Dean Fish

Zoom: 1.500077257046865e-10,9.412807053770777e-11
Location: 0.271733734210405,0.0048881670741758015
Iterations: 3040

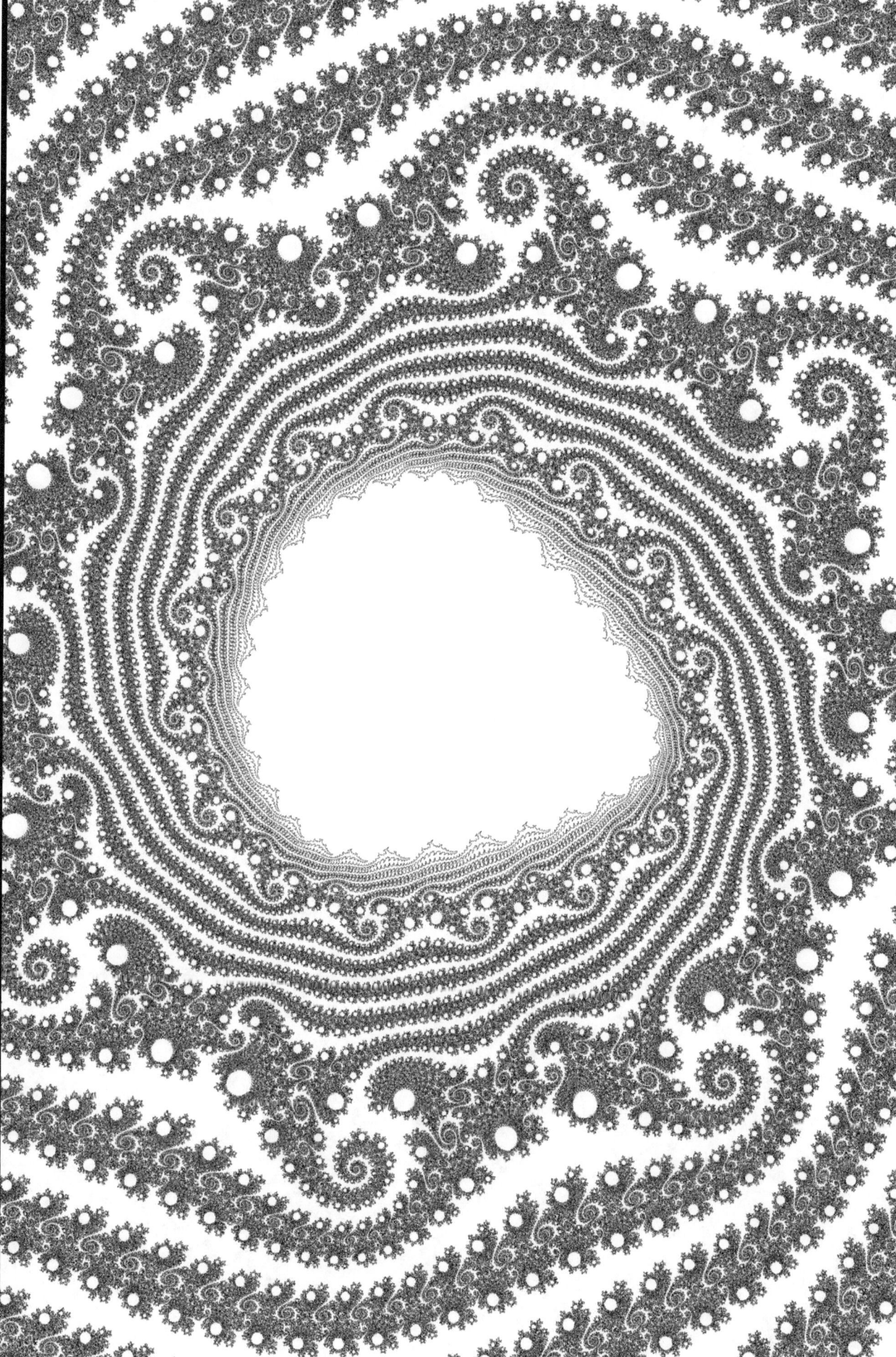

Spindly Spiral In

Zoom: 1.7965811769774274e-10,1.1273334022469248e-10
Location: -0.3466150948067195,0.6067610725166125
Iterations: 3435

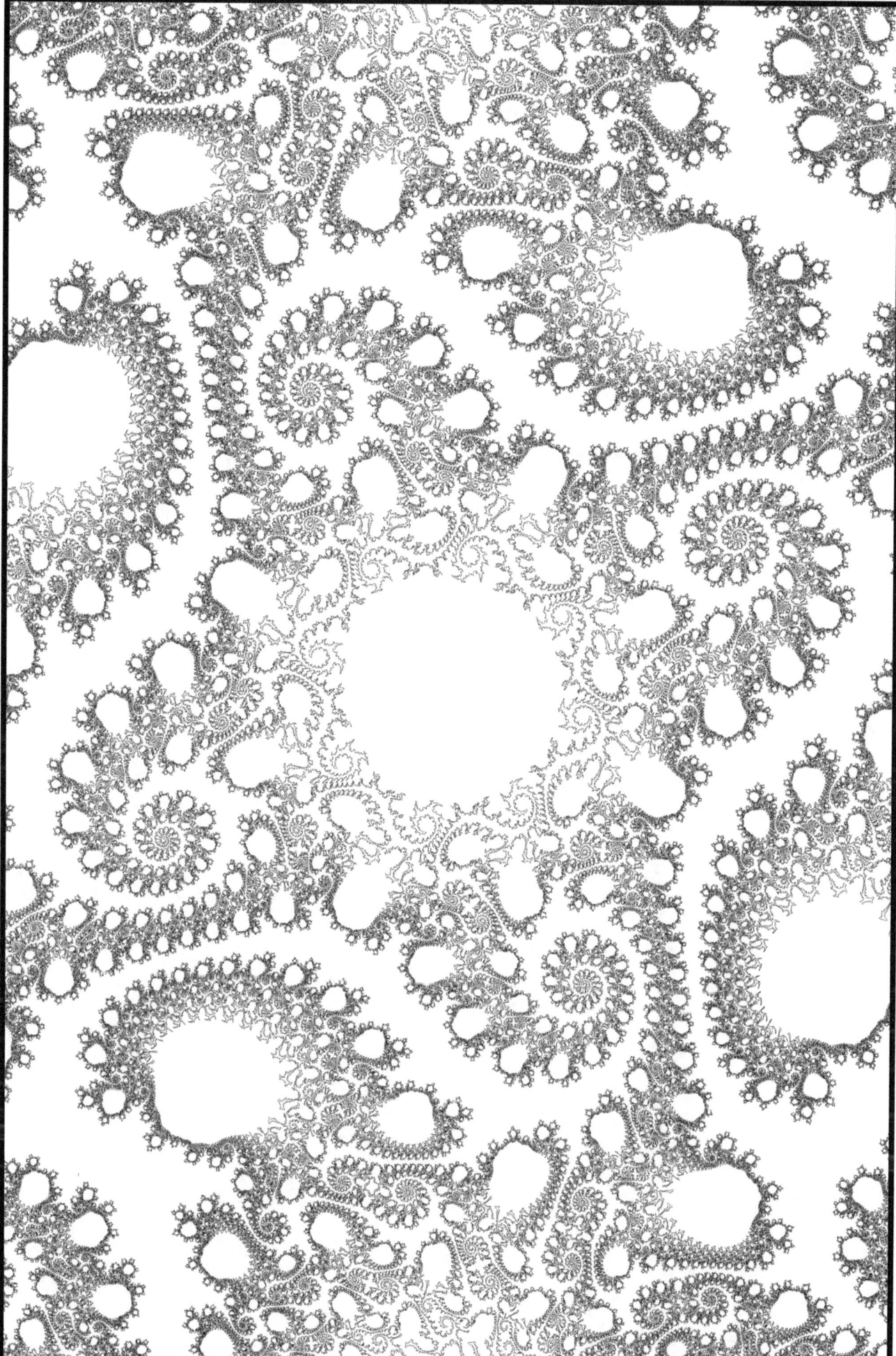

Spindly Spiral Stuff Four

Zoom: 0.000001023849303963691,6.42453307334304e-7
Location: -0.34710313470457593,0.606511677981467
Iterations: 1200

She Sells

Zoom: 2.0494304238185363e-7,1.2859933085934063e-7
Location: -0.7602406722202416,-0.08452578734197504
Iterations: 770

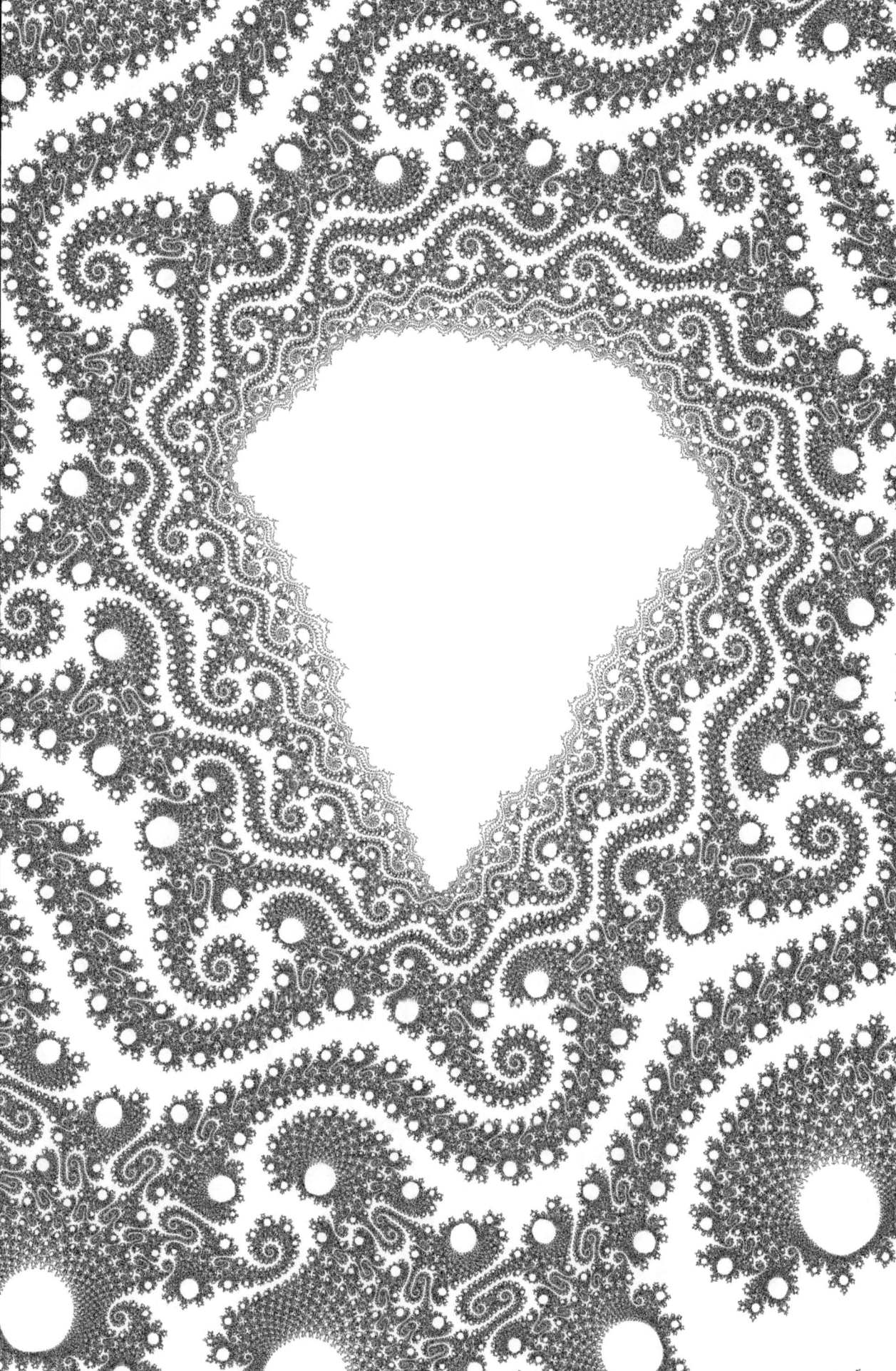

Super Spindly

Zoom: 2.207415569577099e-7,1.3851271156967294e-7
Location: -0.3466106033927194,0.6067781815980282
Iterations: 1835

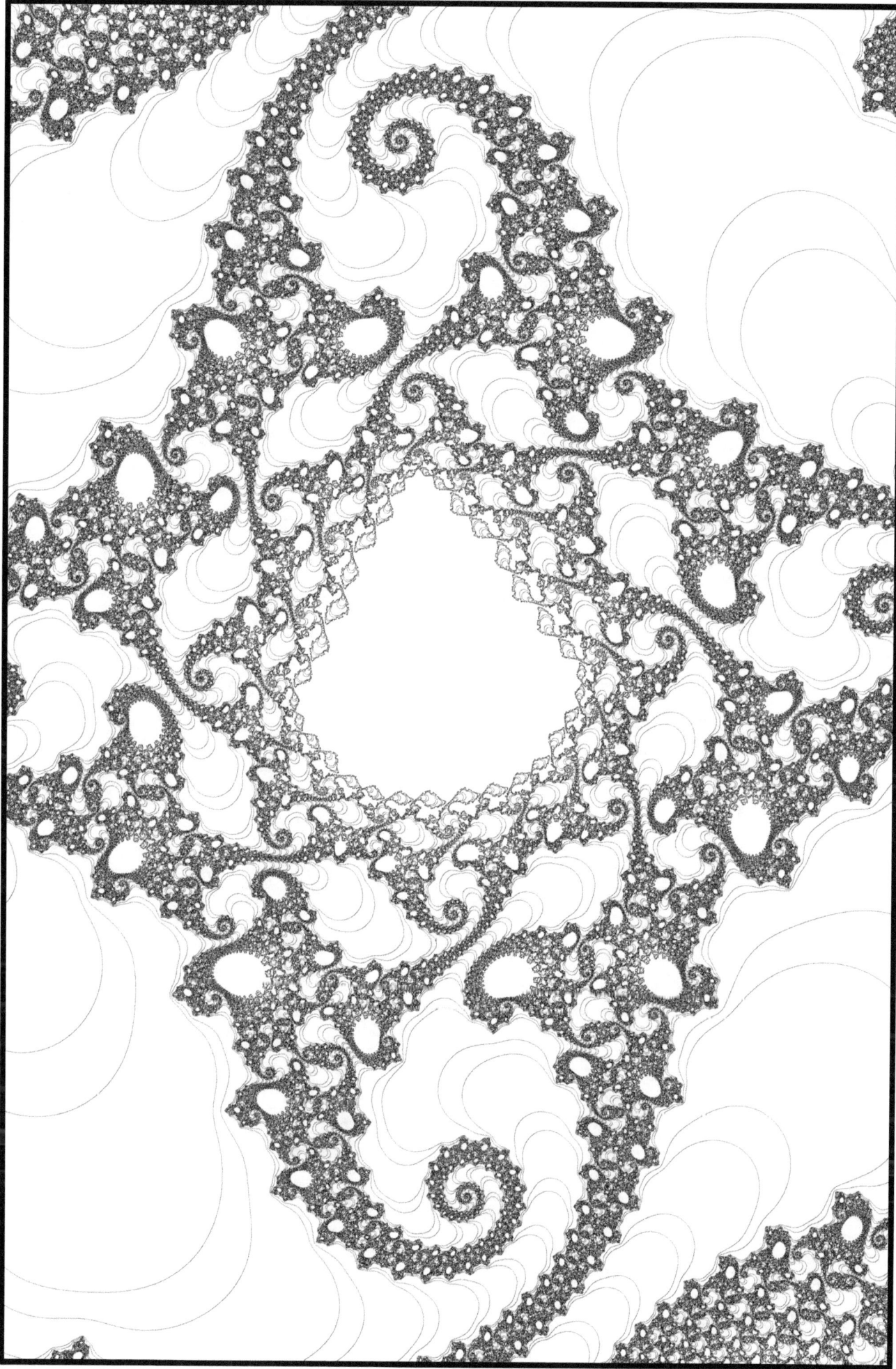

ColorBook 3

Zoom: 0.000011473675371732735,0.00005720038746815116
Location: -0.7468499421937187,0.08759548667154615
Iterations: 440

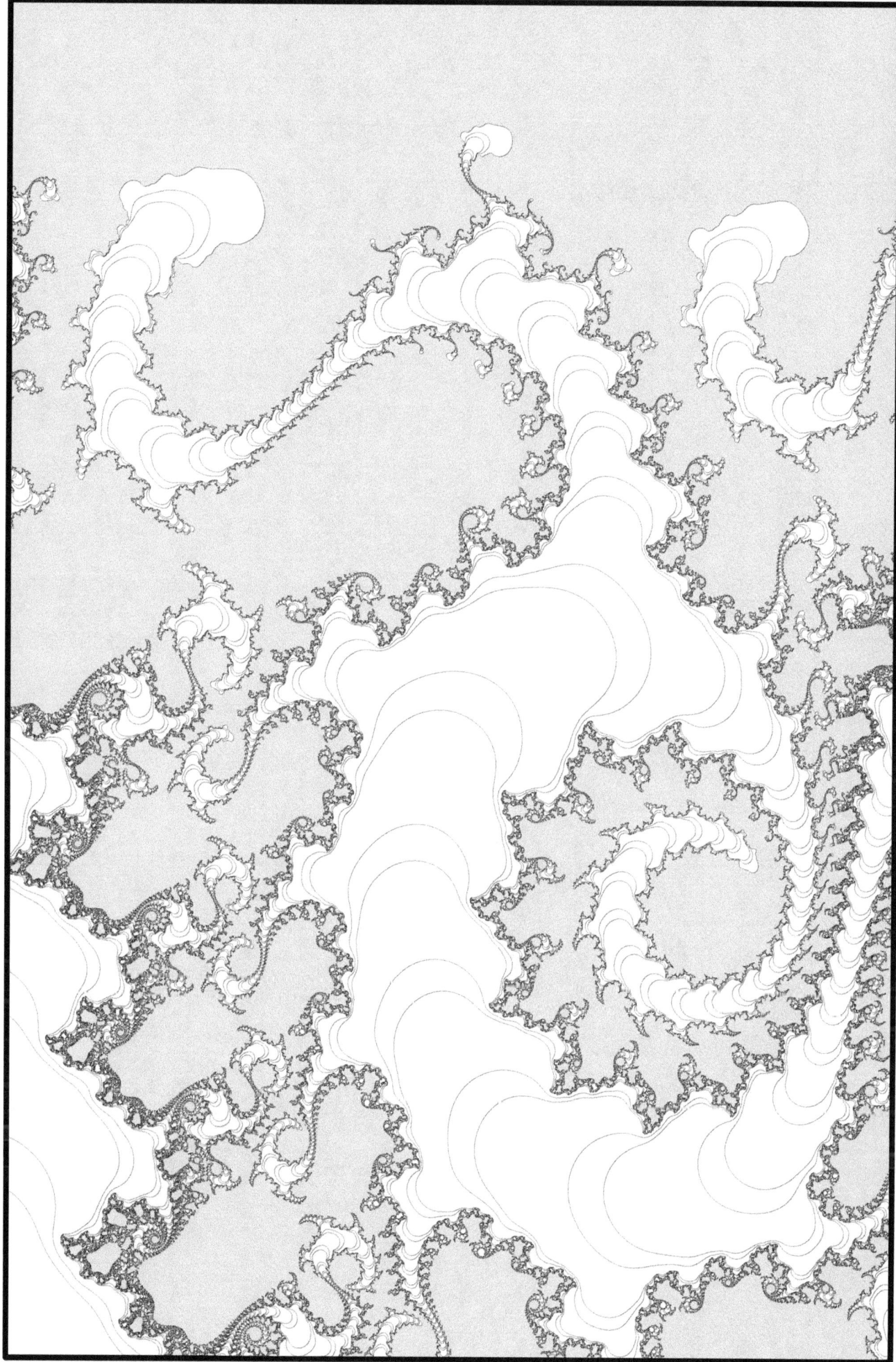

Stripe Dragon 2

Zoom: 3.1923091358932525e-7,2.0031361592442773e-7
Location: 0.2404497431087928,0.5099445000076531
Iterations: 600

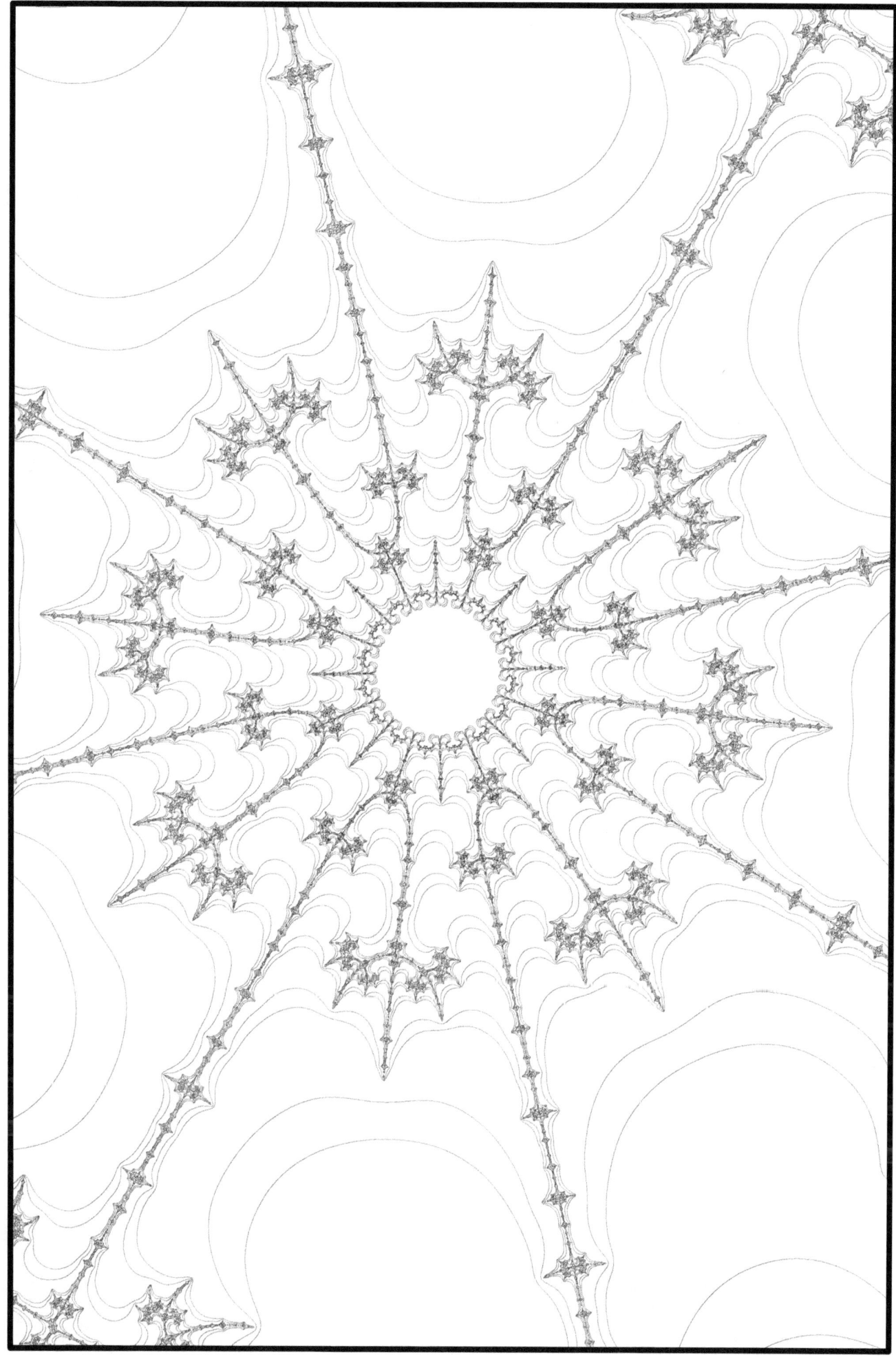

Nobs 3

Zoom: 1.7965486542055106e-10,1.1273117823110767e-10
Location: -1.740032678994083,0.000013742125037621045
Iterations: 140

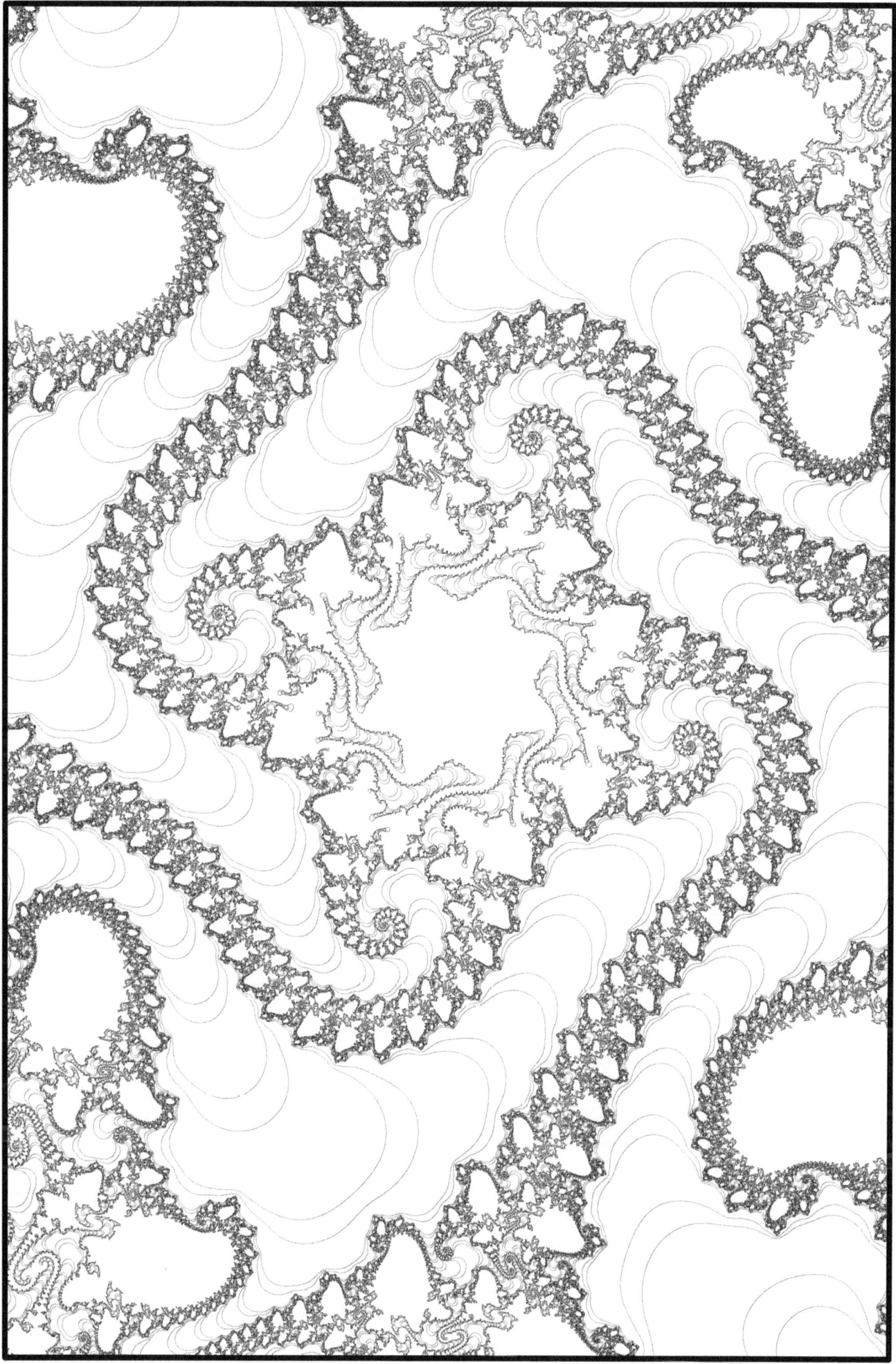

Tails Entwine Zoom

Zoom: 5.013766285943413e-7,3.1460789394831333e-7
Location: -0.7424945231042993,0.11087019475463979
Iterations: 421

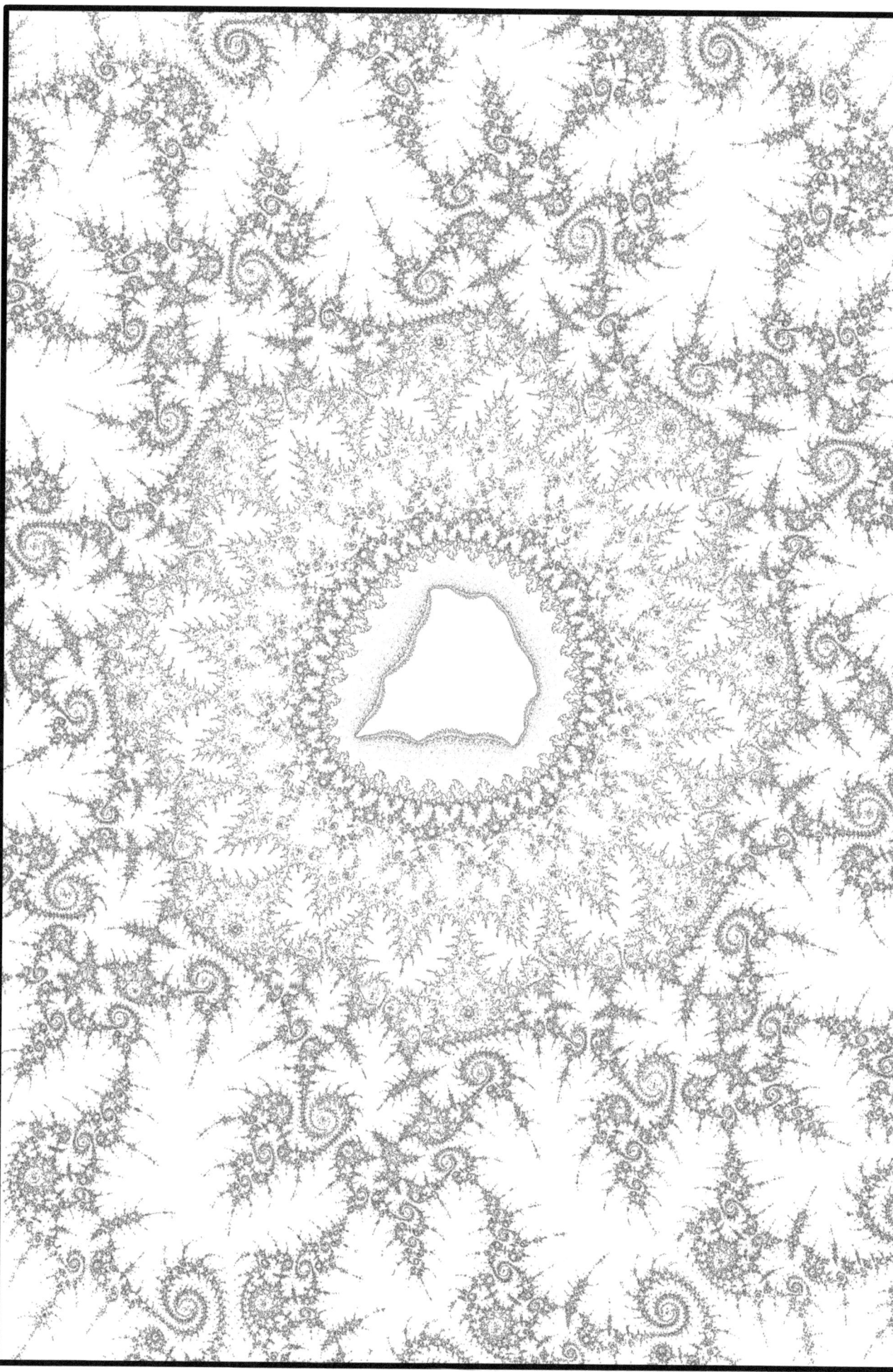

Inside Prickle 2

Zoom: 4.61501104004013e-12.2.3007485494887546e-12
Location: -1.3691652371759793,-0.006555815741688641
Iterations: 3747

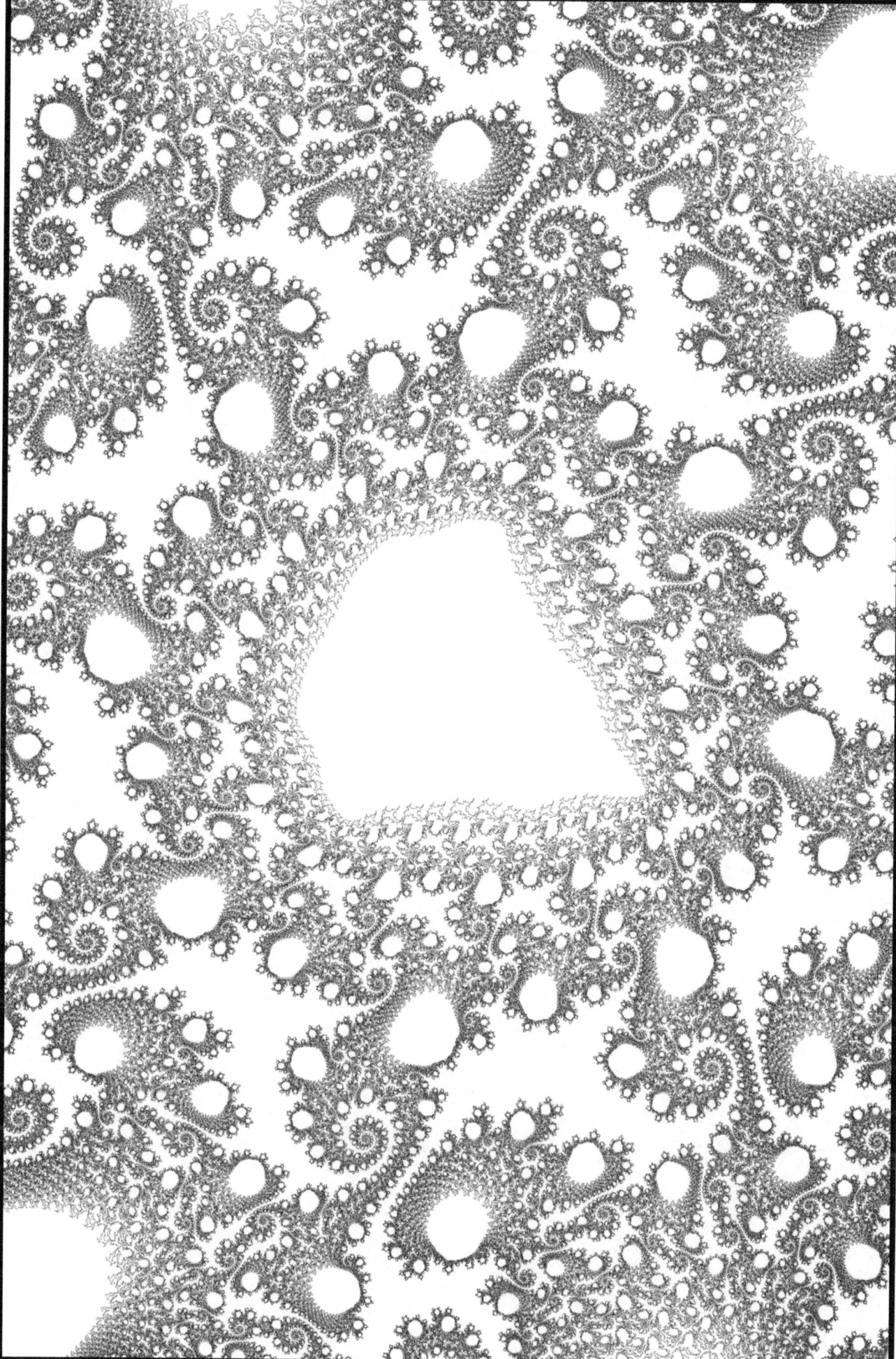

Spindly Hole

Zoom: 5.6169758035394445e-8,3.524585532004082e-8
Location: -0.3470788106081745,0.6064892595132915
Iterations: 1435

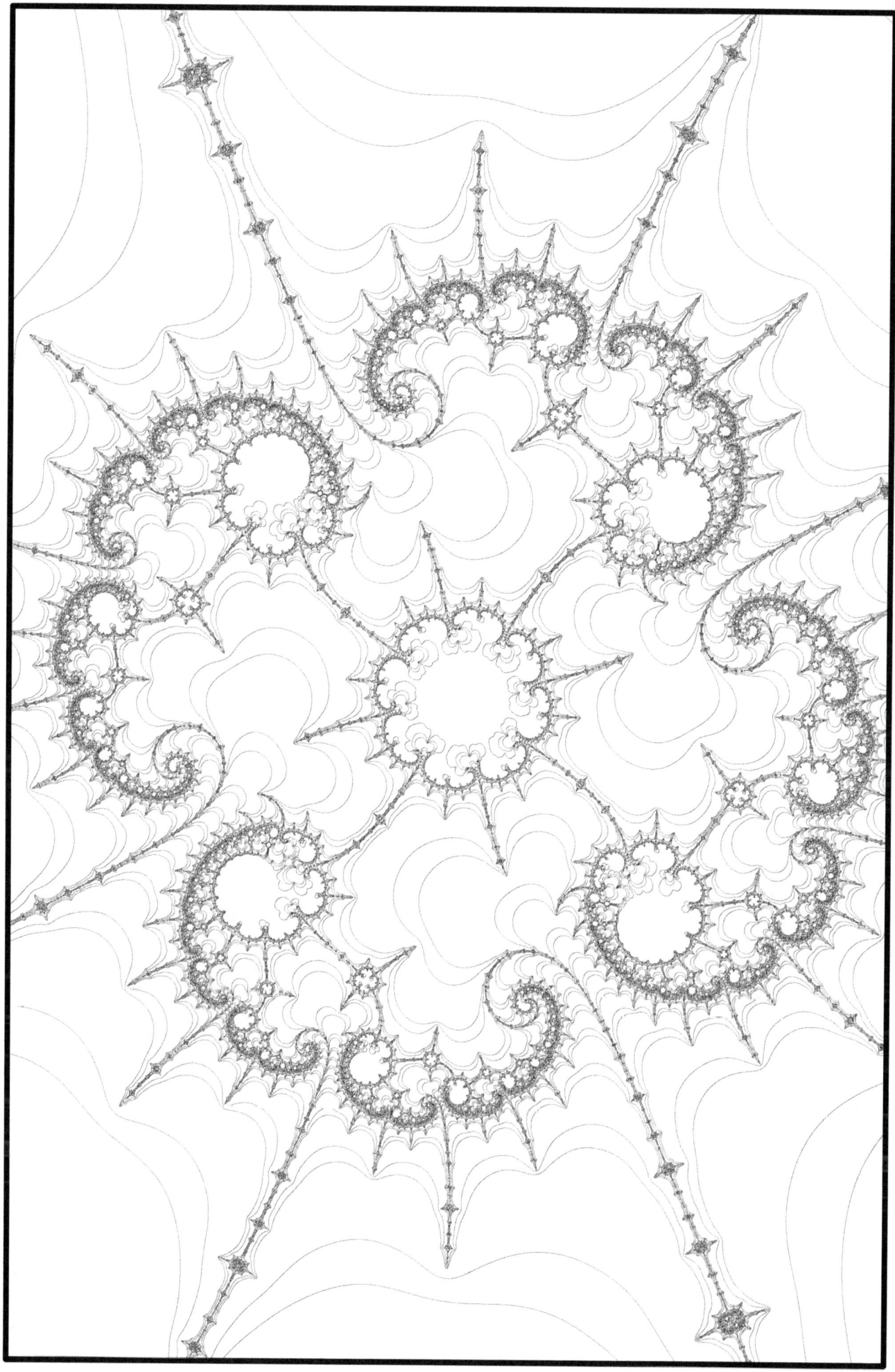

Nobs 8

Zoom: 5.269792184547527e-7,3.306732156626632e-7
Location: -1.7488479341537975,-0.0003104223093106774
Iterations: 170

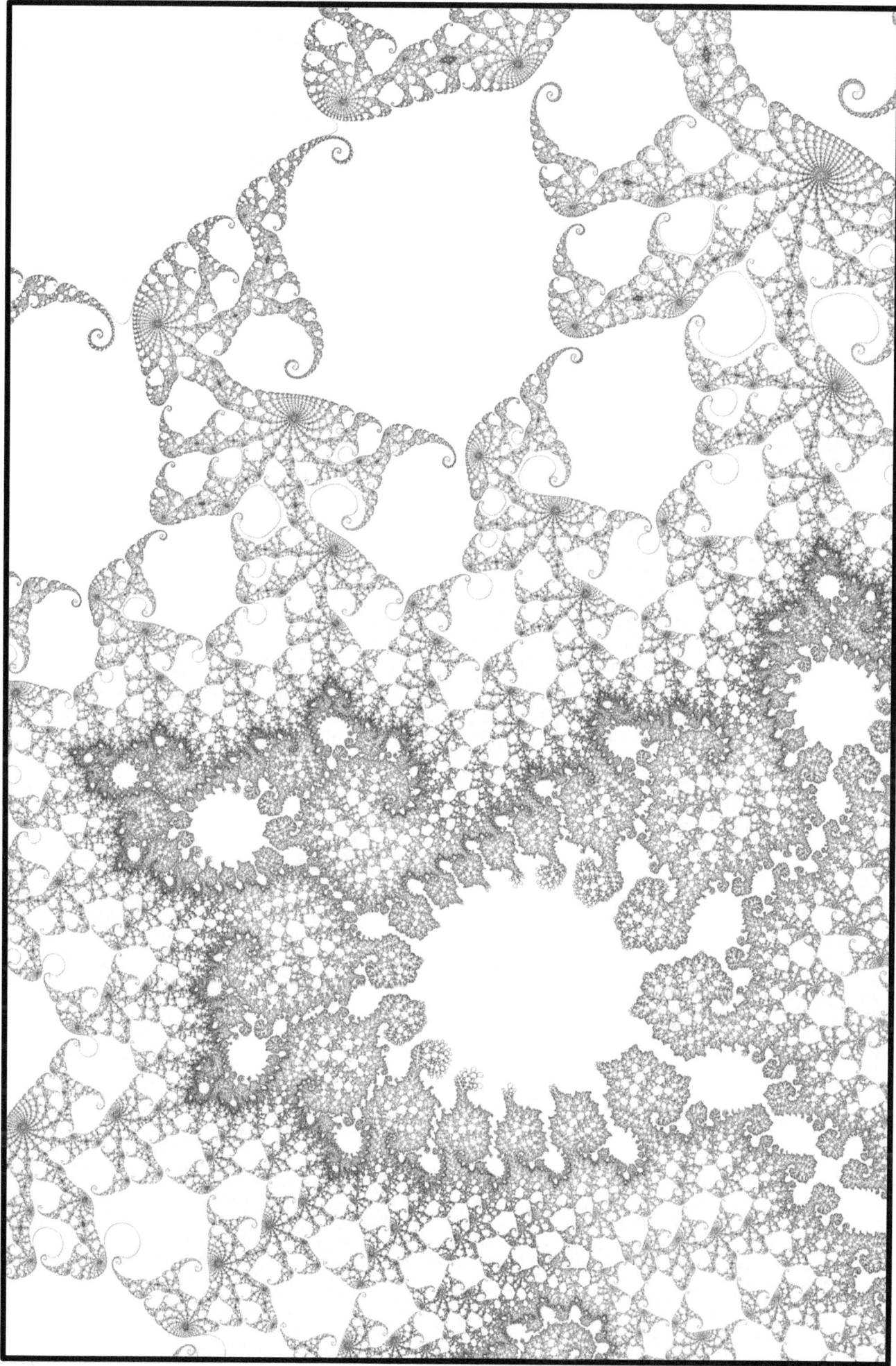

Ant Walk

Zoom: 1.3394772268020326e-8,8.40506089235343e-9
Location: 0.2717356260140749,0.004888612393516441
Iterations: 1400

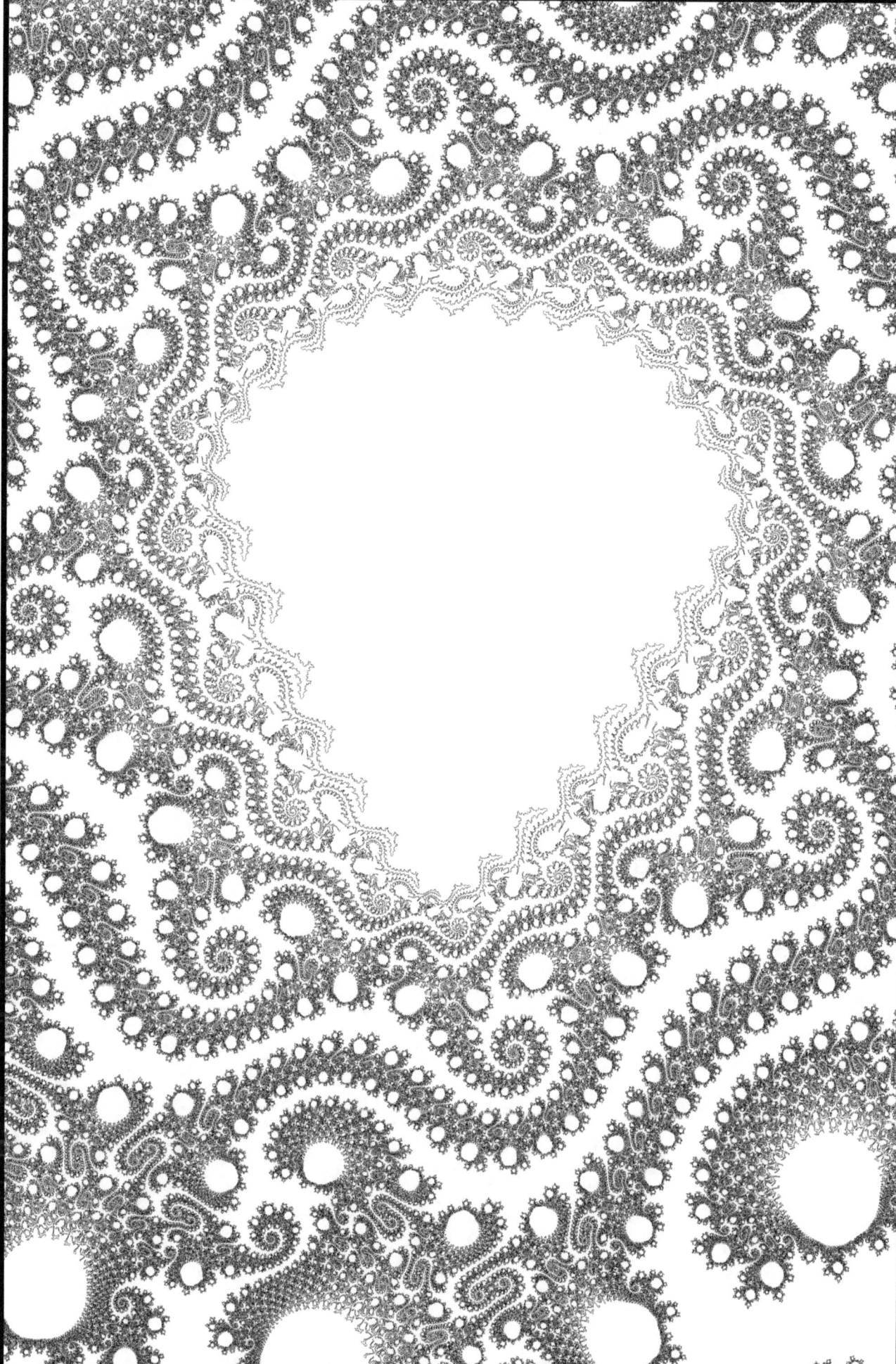

Super Spindly

Zoom: 2.207415569577099e-7,1.3851271156967294e-7
Location: -0.3466106033927194,0.6067781815980282
Iterations: 1535

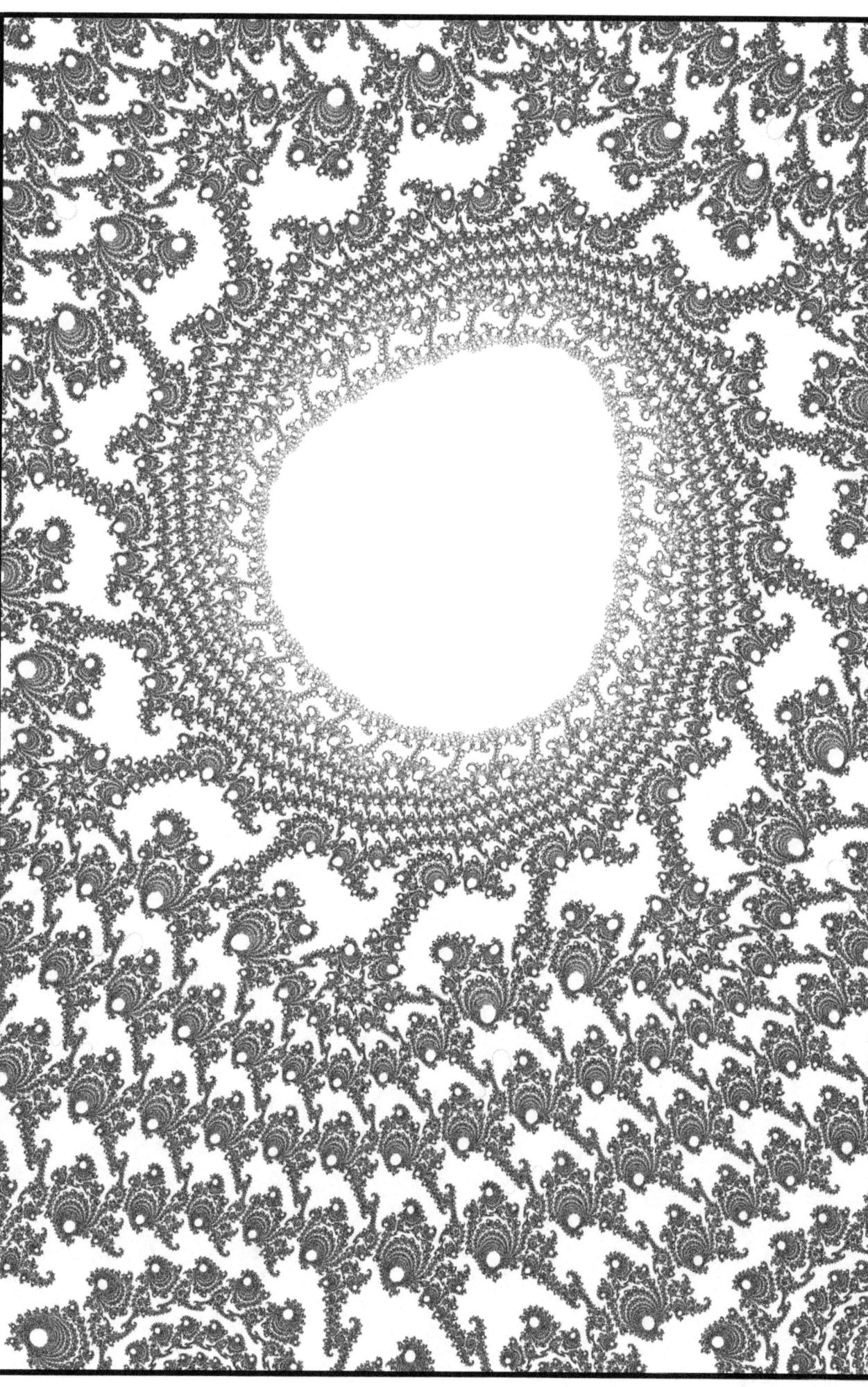

Million Slugs

Zoom: 2.00578375957859e-11,1.2586034828920555e-11
Location: -0.7244238529394607,0.18555240327269637
Iterations: 2923

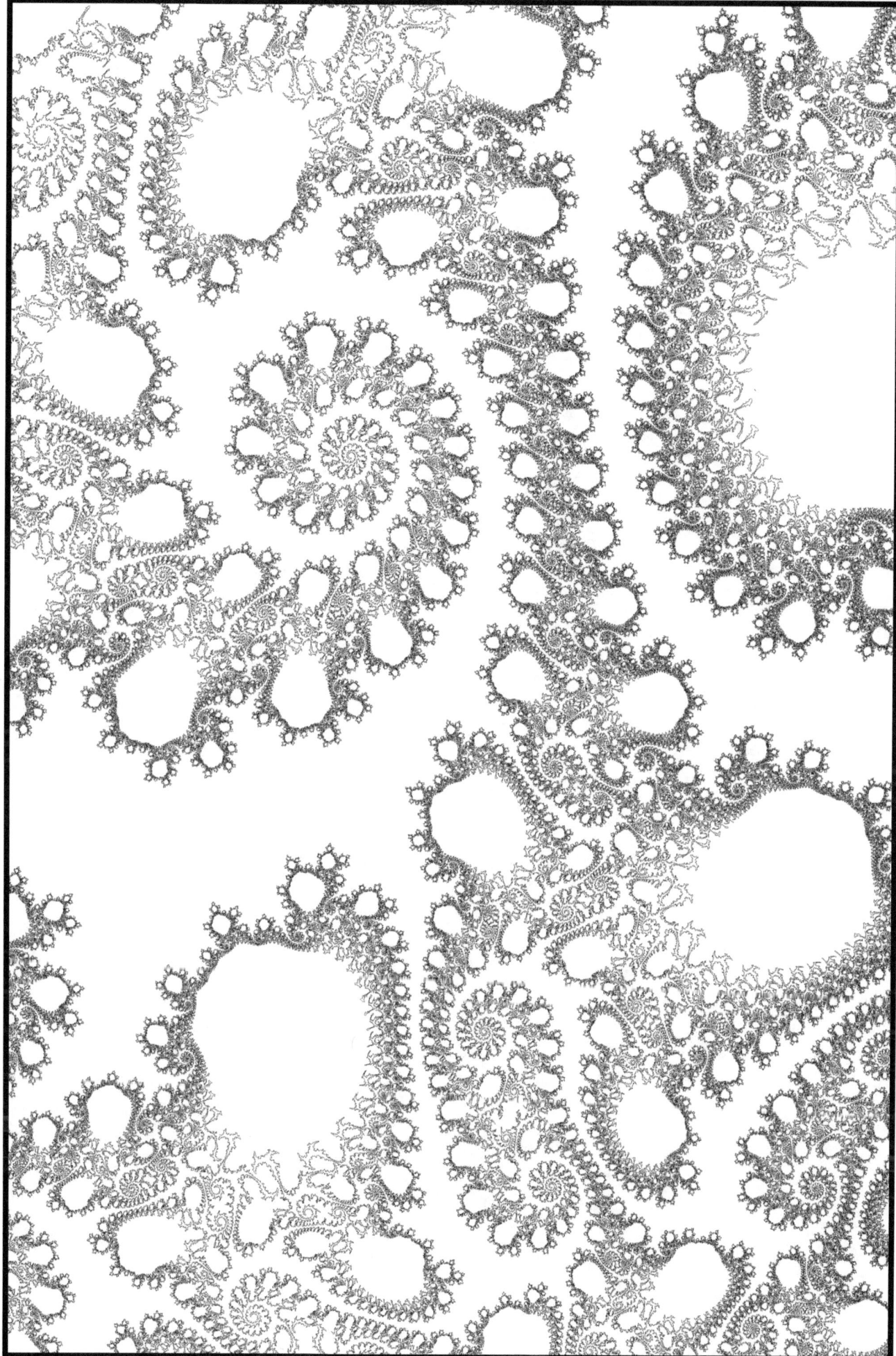

Spindly Spiral Stuff Too

Zoom: 0.0000011930353270608138,7.486155322561652e-7
Location: -0.3471021650569229,0.606503702119788
Iterations: 1035

Inside Prickle 1

Zoom: 4.61501104004013e-12,2.3007485494887546e-12
Location: -1.3691652371759793,-0.006555815741688641
Iterations: 1849

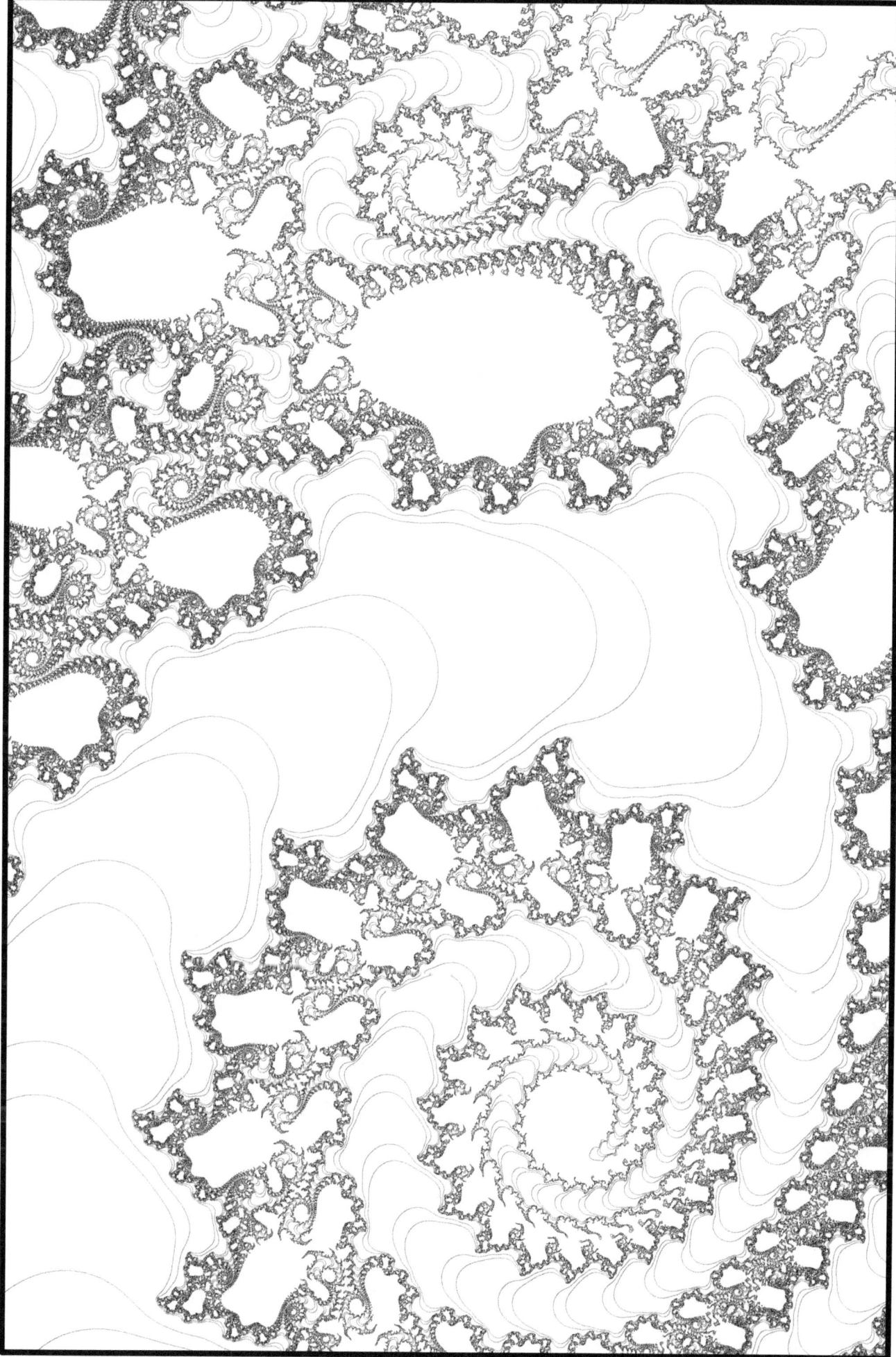

Stripe Dragon 3

Zoom: 8.344799402006953e-7,5.236262752998053e-7
Location: 0.24044946116353447,0.5099442174793805
Iterations: 600

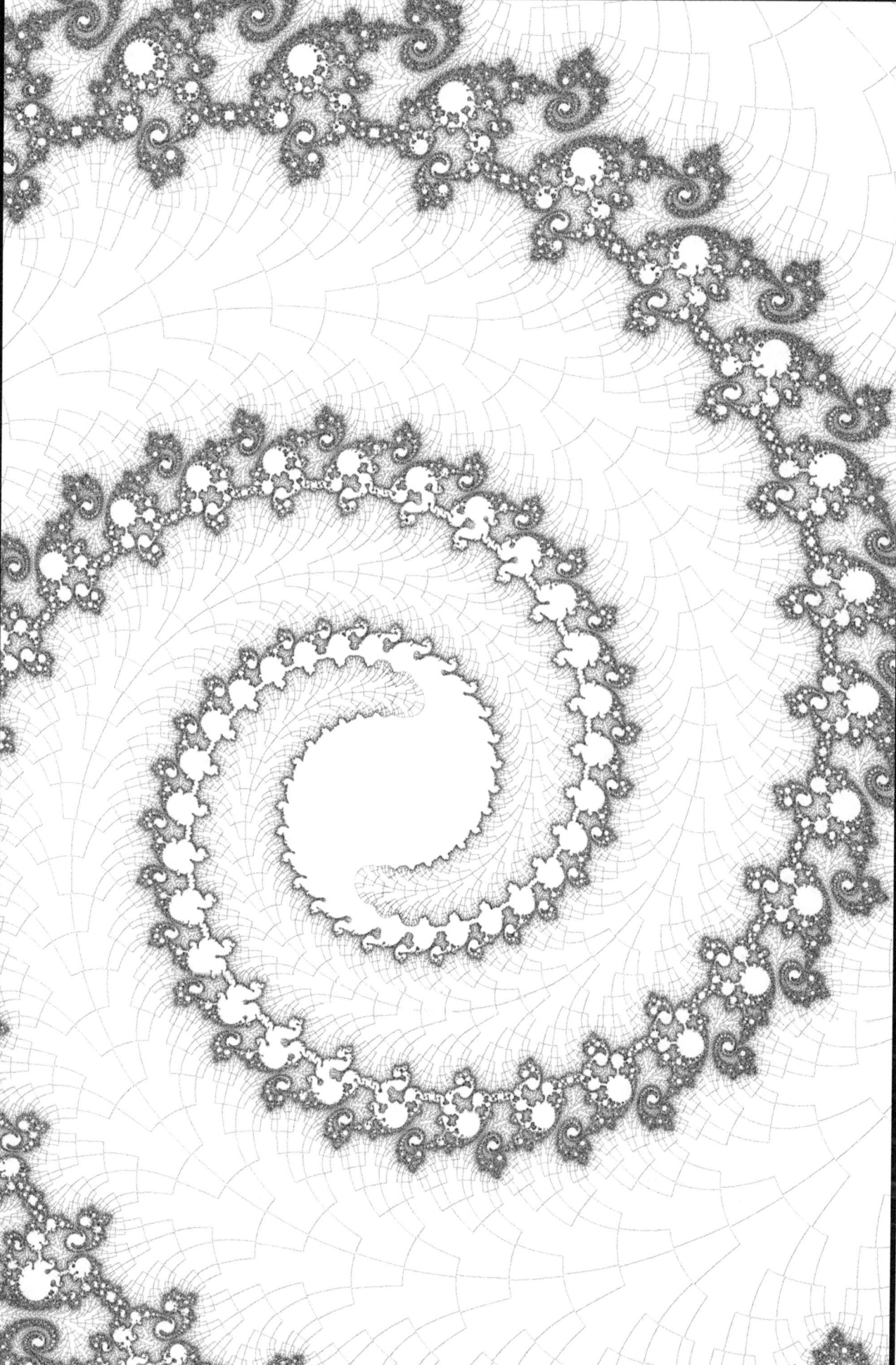

Spiral Feathers

Zoom: 0.00000425415404481008,0.0000026694312582493787
Location: -0.7687151401103818,0.11206490596581477
Iterations: 260

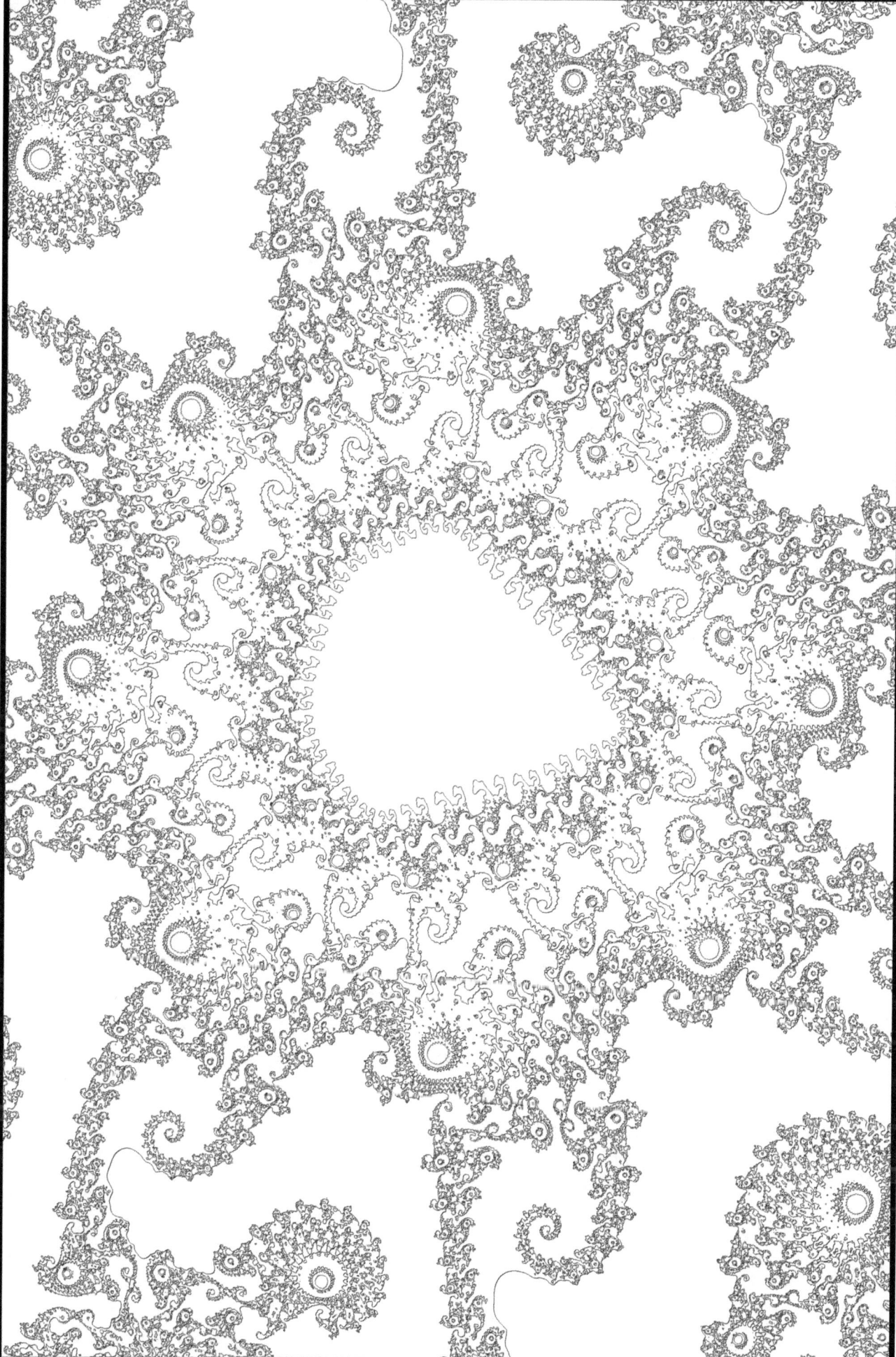

Paisley Fish Eggs

Zoom: 3.559251317622112e-8,2.2333880349147793e-8
Location: -0.7453519917260227,-0.11312356832661097
Iterations: 870

www.ingramcontent.com/pod-product-compliance
Lightning Source LLC
Chambersburg PA
CBHW080710190526
45169CB00006B/2319